Public Relations for Asia

PUBLIC RELATIONS FOR ASIA

Trevor Morris
and
Simon Goldsworthy

palgrave
macmillan

First published in 2008 by
PALGRAVE MACMILLAN
Houndmills, Basingstoke, Hampshire RG21 6XS and
175 Fifth Avenue, New York, N.Y. 10010
Companies and representatives throughout the world.

PALGRAVE MACMILLAN is the global academic imprint of the Palgrave Macmillan division of St. Martin's Press, LLC and of Palgrave Macmillan Ltd. Macmillan® is a registered trademark in the United States, United Kingdom and other countries. Palgrave is a registered trademark in the European Union and other countries.

ISBN-13: 978–0–230–54941–8
ISBN-10: 0–230–54941–1

This book is printed on paper suitable for recycling and made from fully managed and sustained forest sources. Logging, pulping and manufacturing processes are expected to conform to the environmental regulations of the country of origin.

A catalogue record for this book is available from the British Library.

A catalog record for this book is available from the Library of Congress.

10 9 8 7 6 5 4 3 2 1
17 16 15 14 13 12 11 10 09 08

Printed and bound in China

Contents

Part II   Strategy and Planning

Contents

Preface

This book has its origins in our experience of teaching Public Relations (PR) to students from all parts of Asia at the University of Westminster in London. All education should be a stimulating experience – for teachers as well as for those they teach – and for us this was very much the case on our PR courses. Our interaction with students from China, India and from many other countries in the region continues to give us plenty of food for thought about the nature of PR work in Asia.

"Public Relations" – under that title – may be a relative newcomer to the region, even if many of the techniques associated with it have been embedded in traditional cultures since ancient times. What is clear is that, however late their beginnings, the new PR industries across Asia are now growing at a furious pace. The latest techniques in PR are needed not just for domestic commercial reasons, or to further public policy goals, but to meet new international demands, as Asian markets receive unprecedented amounts of foreign investment and as Asian companies increasingly become players in their own right in the international market place. The emergence of strong Asian brands will demand strong PR support in the global marketplace. Key-note events – the Beijing Olympics, the Commonwealth Games in Delhi in 2010 and the Shanghai Expo in the same year, to name but three – are attracting enormous publicity and interest and impose unprecedented PR demands. They are also pointers to an exciting but challenging future.

The youthfulness of the PR industry in much of Asia is also apparent. What we read confirms what we see for ourselves: PR practitioners in Asia are – literally – young. In the space of half a generation or less PR has become a popular career choice and PR courses are very much in demand. All of this makes for great vibrancy, and allows great scope for innovation, but it also means that there has been – understandably – little time to accumulate knowledge and experience. It leaves PR people at risk of appearing unprepared to advise senior executives and unable to deal with big problems and opportunities. This predicament must be avoided.

All of this led us to think that a book which drew upon our experience as PR educators and practitioners and explained the fundamental principles of Public Relations work would be helpful. We have tried to put contemporary PR work into context, so that you can understand the key issues under discussion in the industry. We have also tried to show, through examples and case studies, how the tried and tested principles of PR might be applied to the needs of your country, or the countries where you plan to work. However *you* are best placed to take account of everything that is distinctive about your country as you go about your day-to-day work: what holds good in one part of Asia will be very different elsewhere. PR work is by definition a profoundly social activity: that, indeed, is one of its great attractions. Your knowledge and insights (including a good understanding of your country's media) are a vital part of what will make you a successful PR person.

Secondly, although we have set out the ways in which you can put together PR strategies and tactics and have explained the key skills that you need to operate as a successful PR person, it would be foolish to deny that true success in PR depends on much more than knowing these principles. Alongside social knowledge and awareness is the other vital ingredient: judgment – the ability to weigh up the information at your disposal and make the right decisions. Reading a book cannot teach you that, but we have tried to help. In the end PR is not about abstract principles, but about how PR techniques can be applied to real-life situations. To gain the maximum benefit from the pages that follow, keep in mind one or more organizations that you know well. If you work in PR already that should not be hard, but even if you do not it should be possible to think about somewhere where you work or study and its PR needs. Scattered through the more practical parts of this book are exercises which you might like to undertake, but for many of them to make sense you will need to think carefully about *your* organization and its PR.

Contact: _morrisgoldsworthy@btinternet.com_
(mailto:morrisgoldsworthy@btinternet.com)

Acknowledgments

A big thanks to some great Public Relations (PR) practitioners whose ideas we have borrowed and adapted, including Francis Hallawell – a truly great trainer in media interview and presentation skills – Chris Lawrence, Hamish Patterson and Jo Carr.

We would also like to thank numerous people from all parts of Asia who have shared with us their knowledge of the challenges and opportunities for the PR industry in their countries. In particular, we are indebted to our students, and above all those from many parts of Asia whom we have taught over the years, and who have in turn taught us about their homelands. We would especially like to mention Yujie He, whose University of Westminster MA dissertation, "Public Relations in China," has been very helpful.

We are grateful to Vesna Goldsworthy for helping to edit the text and to Alja Kranjec for her work on the index.

Finally, we want to thank everyone at Palgrave Macmillan, especially Stephen Rutt and Alexandra Dawe, who helped turn our proposal into reality.

PART I

Understanding Public Relations

Any ambitious person already working in or just starting out in Public Relations (PR) wants – quite rightly – to master the practical skills of PR. But there is more to PR than just the practical skills. You also need to understand the social, business and economic context in which PR operates and be able to map out the main communications issues and construct a logical strategic plan that can be measured and evaluated. While you need to think about the circumstances that prevail in the country where you are working, if you are hoping to reach wider audiences you need to consider the context in other societies as well.

PR careers are – as we shall see – immensely varied. You will want to find the kind of work which suits you. Once you have narrowed down your choice, you will want to impress people at the interview. Being able to demonstrate key practical skills is good, but if you want to get a really good job being able to demonstrate that you have read and thought a bit about PR is even better. Finally, if you want to advance in PR you will need much more than technical skill. Practical skills may get you your first job, but understanding the context in which you are operating and the strategic and communication issues which affect your work will get you your second job.

CHAPTER 1

What is Public Relations?

Public Relations is about persuading people to consent to the purpose of an organization or person. It achieves this – primarily but not exclusively – through the use of media relations.

Since the term *Public Relations* (PR) was first coined over a hundred years ago, some PR people have wrestled with the problem of defining what it means (although it has to be said that the great majority have just got on with their work!). Outsiders – and journalists – have less of a problem. For them PR is overwhelmingly about things like press releases, press conferences and talking to journalists: in two words, *media relations*. Indeed many PR people have job titles such as "press officer" or "press secretary." As we shall see, other activities may well be undertaken by PR people. For example they often create their own, managed media such as company newsletters, brochures and websites, and they set up and run events of different kinds. However such work is not always seen as PR, or done by PR people.

Again, for most outside observers, the purpose of PR is clear enough: it is to persuade people. It might be to persuade people to buy goods and services; to buy (or at least not to sell) shares in a company; to join, contribute to or support a charity; or to vote for a political party. Whatever the objective, PR's task is seen as one of purposeful persuasion.

Our view of PR is similar to that of most outside observers and is reflected in our definition at the start of this section. We believe that media relations work lies at the heart of PR (indeed there probably would not be a PR industry but for the growth of the mass media in modern times) and that PR is about persuading people for a purpose.

We suspect this realistic definition will not bother most people in Asia, but it is worth briefly mentioning some of the alternative views you may find in American and European PR textbooks or on the websites of international PR organizations. Where do these definitions differ from ours?

For the world's largest PR body, the Public Relations Society of America:

> *Public Relations is the professional discipline that ethically fosters mutually beneficial relationships among social entities.*

For Europe's largest PR body, the UK's Chartered Institute of Public Relations:

> *Public Relations is about reputation – the result of what you do, what you say and what others say about you.*
>
> *Public Relations is the discipline which builds and maintains reputation, with the aim of earning understanding and support and influencing opinion and behaviour. It is the planned and sustained effort to establish and maintain goodwill and mutual understanding between an organization and its publics.*

As you will notice, these definitions are quite vague: they tell you little about what PR people actually do all day, and media relations is not mentioned at all. They also avoid using the word "persuasion" and are not very clear about the purposes of PR activity: "mutual understanding" is all very well, but companies have much more precise objectives in mind in terms of increased sales or bettering their position in the financial markets. Charities and politicians also seek to use PR with much more definite objectives than "mutual understanding." They want people to do – or even not do – something. PR people are not neutral referees, but are there to serve the interests of those paying them. Non-PR people might also point out that building and maintaining an organization's reputation is far from being a PR monopoly; instead employees across the organization contribute to the process.

Rather than being genuine and helpful attempts to explain what PR does, too many existing definitions are instead clumsy attempts to avoid issues which some people find awkward. For instance some PR people dislike being labeled as "mere" media relations experts, and prefer to emphasize other aspects of the job. Others shy away from the term "persuasion," which is often seen as being associated with manipulation and seeking to impose one's own will upon others. We suggest that it is in your interests as a PR person to be straightforward about what you do: at least you will not be appearing to dodge the issue! Organizations hire evermore PR people and pay them well because they want to persuade people about various things. They also care about how they are portrayed in the media. They regard all of that as important: if not, why would they pay you?

CHAPTER 2

Lessons from history

The history of Public Relations (PR) may seem irrelevant to the needs of contemporary practitioners, and we do not intend to provide a great deal of it here. However, much of the knowledge which successful PR people use to good effect is drawn from history, even if they have acquired the information informally and certainly do not think of it as "History." There are few, if any, scientific laws in PR. Instead people learn from their own and others' experience of PR work and acquire a knowledge of the industry based on hearing about its ups and downs. Much of what they do today and plan to do tomorrow is based on collective wisdom about what happened yesterday. Some significant themes emerge from PR's history, and some of them are particularly important to understanding the way PR is developing in Asia today. So rather than present a story littered with names and dates, we will simply focus on issues which seem relevant and which will help you understand the present and plan for the future.

Many of the things which make up PR may be timeless, and have existed in Asian societies since the beginnings of human civilization. Businesses have always sought to further their interests, and political and religious leaders have always sought to win and retain support, so "PR" has been part of what people do from time immemorial. However, PR as a specialist field, in which people act in a planned and deliberate way, and to which they devote their working lives, is a relative newcomer. While there will always be important differences between Asia and the North American and European societies where PR as we now know it first emerged, the fact that modern PR developed many decades earlier, in countries like the USA and Britain, means that there may be lessons to learn for societies where PR is newer. No one needs to reinvent the wheel.

"Public Relations" first emerged, under that name, about a hundred years ago in the United States. There was already a well-established tradition of press agents creating publicity in the newspaper press for circuses and other forms of entertainment, but while PR drew on those skills it also represented something new, and something which has interesting parallels with contemporary Asia.

"Guanxi"

There is a natural overlap between Public Relations and the venerable and much older Chinese concept of "Guanxi," which can be very loosely translated as relationships. Guanxi places great emphasis on personal relationships and friendship, and is closely associated with Confucian thought. In consequence it has been argued that Chinese PR people place a little less emphasis on the "public" part of "Public Relations," and more on cultivating more direct, personal relationships. A similar importance is attached to personal relationships in some other countries in Asia. This subtle cultural difference is just one of many that PR practitioners need to bear in mind. It certainly has a great impact on tactical considerations when devising PR plans, although it could be argued that overall PR objectives and strategies tend to be more similar wherever one is in the world.

Source: Adapted from Yujie He's University of Westminster MA thesis

PR and the growth of big business

The large new companies which emerged in the USA just over a century ago increasingly operated in large and growing markets, spread across the North American continent and beyond. The railway companies and mining and oil companies were not only big, with far-flung interests, but were prone to highly publicized crises as accidents occurred or workers took industrial action. Gone were the days when companies could rely on local communities which they knew well and where they were well known. Instead, today's global companies and brands were emerging from provincial America. Procter was ceasing to be a Cincinnati soap manufacturer and becoming what we know as Procter & Gamble, and Coca-Cola was rapidly ceasing to be a small-time medicinal drink manufacturer in the American south. Such businesses needed to start thinking about managing their reputations more carefully, and to start employing professionals to help them do it.

As large businesses of this kind developed, they grew well beyond what an individual entrepreneur or founding family could control. Businessmen had traditionally been jacks of all trades, but increasingly companies came to rely on highly trained professional managers – often accountants, lawyers and engineers – people who respected specialist skills and subdivided work accordingly. Companies saw that they could gain competitive advantage and operate more profitably by building on professional skills in this way.

The same process started to extend to marketing and publicity work, although this is still far from complete in many parts of the world, including many countries in Asia, which is one reason that so many exciting possibilities lie in this field. The US advertising industry began to take its modern shape in the nineteenth century, while the early twentieth century saw the gradual emergence of marketing as a distinct specialism. Businessmen had always been interested in selling their goods and services, but they were now able to do it in a more deliberate and planned way, using staff with special training and experience to help them go about it. They also became used to engaging advertising agencies to help them accomplish their goals. This paved the way for the birth of PR as a specialist business discipline. While PR had always been – and continues to be – part of the portmanteau of skills which marks out the successful entrepreneur or founder of a business, it came increasingly to be entrusted to people with special skills and experience and became a career in its own right.

PR and the mass media

But another factor also served to bring about the birth of modern PR, and it is one that is as relevant to contemporary Asian markets now as it was to American business leaders a hundred years ago.

Late-nineteenth-century America experienced an enormous growth in print journalism, the only mass medium of the day. Many new newspapers and magazines were published, and their circulations soared. For the first time large sections of the population were absorbing the same news and information on a daily basis. Advertising boomed as companies paid to exploit the opportunities this created to reach mass audiences in new ways. However, advertisements had inherent drawbacks: not only were they costly, but also everyone knew who was behind them; however clever the ad, it was always a company singing its own praises.

Press agents, in many ways the precursors of PR in America, took advantage of the opportunities this created. They recognized that journalists had needs of their own – that they wanted interesting and newsworthy material with which to fill their pages. Press agents could supply the material, but did so on behalf of the companies who hired them, making sure that the story provided a favorable namecheck or mention for their paymaster. Not only was this "free" publicity (the press agent had to be paid, but the journalist and the newspaper did not), but it also offered an additional advantage. Rather than appearing in the form of an advertisement, the information appeared on the printed page as editorial content, written by an independent journalist and bearing the independent authority of the publication in which it featured. As we all know, anyone can claim they are good at something, but it is much more credible if someone else – someone who is independent – says they are. This special quality, called "**third party endorsement**," remains the strongest unique selling proposition for PR. To use a simple but effective analogy, advertising is like walking into a meeting and telling the people present, "I am very good at what I do." PR is like walking into that meeting and some of the people telling the others you are very good at what you do!

Although the emerging mass media created new opportunities to put across favorable messages, they also represented a threat. The new mass circulation newspapers were competing with others to sell copies and, as any journalist will confirm, bad news and stories about conflict and crises tend to sell better than good news. Hostile stories not only made unpleasant reading for businesspeople but could also lead to a loss of custom, undermine share prices or lead to calls for government action. By the early twentieth century, in an era of growing democratic accountability, US business felt increasingly beleaguered. The new big corporations were obvious targets. Businesspeople started to feel it was worth paying to halt, or at least minimize, negative press coverage. Ideally media interest in big business could even be turned around and transformed into positive coverage. It was perhaps this, more than anything, that first gave rise to the modern PR industry.

If PR was born out of developments in journalism, it is also worth noting that many of its first practitioners were themselves former journalists who were able to exploit their knowledge of how the media work. They understood what makes a good story, and what does not, and they knew the pressures under which a journalist works. This established a tradition which continues to this day: many PR practitioners, including some of the most senior, formerly worked in journalism, and their understanding of the media is greatly valued. PR continues to provide an alternative career for journalists, one which often offers better pay and working conditions. There is also the opportunity to set up a business independently by establishing a PR consultancy.

Today Asia is a continent where – in many countries – newspaper circulations are still increasing (whereas in much of the West they are in gentle decline). The media in all their forms are on the rise, and there are increased demands for accountability on the part of rapidly expanding businesses and governments. While history may not repeat itself exactly, current patterns of development augur well for the rise of PR in Asia.

Recent developments

Since the 1980s the developed world's PR industry has enjoyed unprecedented levels of growth, much faster than the economy generally. The reasons for this are highly relevant for Asia, which has already been through many of the same experiences. Market liberalization, as promoted by President Reagan and UK Prime Minister Margaret Thatcher in the 1980s, created enormous needs for PR services. The privatization of state assets – nationalized industries – by selling shares involved expensive PR campaigns. The competing companies or regulated businesses which emerged from the privatization process became much greater users of PR than their nationalized predecessors, as they actively sought business, endeavored to please their shareholders and lobbied government and regulators.

All of this gave an enormous boost to PR, beginning with financial PR specialists, but quickly spreading to all parts of the PR industry. The economic growth with which this liberalization was associated coincided with a consumer boom, leading to new opportunities for many kinds of PR as people shopped more, traveled more and enjoyed an ever wider range of expensive leisure pursuits. While advertising continued (and continues) to play an important part in promoting the sale of goods and services, spending in the evermore affluent societies of the West was increasingly lavished on big-ticket items – cars, property, luxury holidays, financial services – where simply relying on the advertiser's own words was insufficient. People could not simply sample these goods and services at minimal cost and then decide whether to make a repeat purchase. Instead people seemed to want these products subjected to independent critical review by journalists. At the same time growing volumes of media content – thicker newspapers with more supplements, more magazines and increasing amounts of broadcast programming, all produced without any commensurate increase in numbers of journalists – created unprecedented opportunities for PR.

CHAPTER 3

The structure of the PR industry

Public Relations (PR) work is today undertaken both "in-house" – by an organization's own employees, who form a PR or communications department – and by PR consultancies or agencies, independent businesses which hire out their services to a range of employers. This split character, which applies globally and has always been a feature of the industry, contrasts with the business disciplines with which PR is most closely associated. Advertising is overwhelmingly handled by independent agencies: few organizations, even the very largest, seek to create their own advertisements or buy media space. And, while marketing consultancies exist, marketing tends to be seen more firmly as a core discipline and handled in-house.

Increasingly in Western economies the in-house or directly employed arm of the PR industry predominates in terms of the numbers of people employed. Most organizations of any size now expect to have their own PR departments, whereas many used to rely on consultancies for all PR-related work. In-house PR departments – with a range of different titles (communications, corporate communications, corporate affairs, external affairs) – have spread well beyond big business and central government to medium sized businesses, small government bodies and not-for-profit organizations such as charities and educational organizations. This reflects the increased acceptance of PR as an important tool which should be at the heart of an organization and at its constant disposal. Moreover, if used constantly, on a day-to-day basis, PR is usually carried out more cheaply by directly employed staff than by outside contractors who have to add their own profit margin. In-house PR teams are usually quite small relative to the organizations that employ them, and their budgets are also relatively low. Their importance lies elsewhere: they are usually at the forefront of whatever problems or challenges their organizations face, and often enjoy unrivaled access to the chief executive and other senior managers because of their media-handling skills.

Independent PR consultancies may only employ a minority of all PR people but have tended to have a higher profile than the in-house teams. In industry circles at least, big firms such as Burson Marsteller and Hill & Knowlton are well known internationally, and traditionally their senior staff got more coverage in the trade press – and beyond – than their in-house counterparts. This is now changing as in-house heads of PR become more prominent. However, despite the spread of in-house PR, consultancies continue to thrive. Increasingly they run specific PR campaigns or help with individual projects rather than run all aspects of an organization's PR. They can offer particular skills and capabilities which are not available to an in-house PR team and which can be more economically supplied by specialists who are called in when and as required.

Such consultancies come in many shapes and sizes. A few – including the best known ones – are big, international firms with offices in many countries. Such firms are well represented across Asia. Many more are much smaller, operating in one location for a few clients. In practice all but the biggest consultancies tend to specialize in some way. It may be that they generally work for a particular kind of client – fashion, music, consumer, healthcare or IT companies, for example – or that their expertise lies in a particular kind of PR. For example, any organization facing possible problems from planned government legislation might call in a lobbying or public affairs specialist, whereas companies involved in mergers or takeovers typically use financial PR specialists. There are also firms which specialize in internal communications, crisis management and in media evaluation, a discipline which seeks to measure the impact of PR.

At its lower end the consultancy scene has always been highly changeable and dynamic, moving swiftly to seize opportunities and meet new needs. In most societies there are few barriers to setting up a PR consultancy, and little capital is required. Indeed the openness and flexibility of the PR consultancy world has always been one of its attractions. Frequently, PR people from existing consultancies or in-house teams, or indeed journalists, set up PR firms of their own. While plenty fall by the wayside, some succeed and grow very rapidly. They are then often bought by larger, better-established firms.

Many of the large international PR firms can trace their origins to the early decades of PR in America in the twentieth century and still retain the names of their original founders and owners. However, over recent decades they have largely ceased to be independent businesses. Instead, most have become subsidiaries within the handful of international marketing services groups, such as WPP and Interpublic, holding firms which bring together the best-known advertising agencies as well as other marketing disciplines (such as research) under common ownership (see Table 3.1).

Table 3.1

Major international communications/marketing services groups			
Name of holding company	Nationality	Main PR companies owned by group	Some key advertising companies owned by group
Interpublic	US	Weber Shandwick, GolinHarris	McCann Erickson
WPP	UK	Hill & Knowlton, Burson-Marsteller, Ogilvy PR, Cohn & Wolfe, 24% stake in Chime	Young & Rubicam, J Walter Thompson, Ogilvy & Mather, Grey Global Group
Omnicom	US	Ketchum, Porter Novelli, Fleishman-Hillard	BBDO Worldwide, DDB Worldwide, TBWA Worldwide
Publicis	French	Manning, Selvage & Lee, Rowland, Freud Communications	Saatchi & Saatchi, Leo Burnett, Publicis
Havas	French	Euro RSCG, Biss Lancaster, Maitland	Euro RSCG, Arnold Worlwide

Big consultancies typically offer a wide range of PR services, with specialist staff offering advice on, for example, business-to-business communication, marketing PR with the aim of selling consumer goods, lobbying or public affairs, and internal communications (see below for details of these specialisms) – to name but a few of the services on offer. This can offer clients the benefit of enjoying a seamless service, with all their PR needs being met and coordinated under one roof. However, as mentioned, plenty of smaller consultancies continue to emerge, often run by senior staff who have broken away from larger agencies, and they often focus on a particular area of business in which they have developed particular expertise.

Hill & Knowlton in China

Hill & Knowlton, historically one of the world's largest PR consultancies, was the first international PR firm to set up in China, in 1984. Its global CEO, Paul Taaffe, has commented that its early years in China involved educating the marketplace about Public Relations, and for the first 10–15 years it was largely concerned with introducing foreign companies into the Chinese market. Overseas corporations found it easier to rely on outsourced PR before they brought in their own staff. Now, as the branches of big PR consultancies spread across China, he comments:

"If you want to be in the global communications business and you're not in China you're not a player."

Source: PR Week podcast

CHAPTER 4

PR and integrated marketing communications

Much of Public Relations (PR) is about helping to sell goods and services. Called "marketing PR," it is very much about marketing communications or "marcoms," rather than about some of the wider issues with which PR concerns itself. Typically such PR activity, which may be undertaken in-house or by consultants, is controlled by the marketing director of a company and is usually undertaken in conjunction with other persuasive disciplines, such as advertising and sales promotions.

These disciplines can generally be distinguished from each other. Advertising, for example, involves using paid-for space in the media and elsewhere, and traditionally such space is clearly distinguished from editorial space which is where PR aims to gain coverage (thus PR might be seeking a favorable mention within a TV news program, but advertising appears in the commercial breaks before, during or after the program).[1] Sales promotions represent incentives to buy particular products (buy one, get one free; or money off coupons). However in marketing they are all used in concert, in pursuit of common objectives and the greater good of the organization. Properly done this constitutes "integrated marketing communications" (IMC), and the new marketing services groups such as WPP and Interpublic are designed to offer all these different services in a coordinated way.

In practice reality can stop short of the ideal, not least because of human nature. Because these different disciplines have grown up separately, there are professional rivalries and perhaps inhibitions about admitting the importance of other aspects of IMC. Nor is it just vanity – budgets and money are at stake. If, from a given budget, more is spent on one of these disciplines then less must be spent on the others, a fact of life which can lead to friction.

The need for PR within the marketing mix

Cadbury's controversial Indian ad for its Temptations chocolate bar suggested the disputed Kashmir region between India and Pakistan is – like the chocolate bar – "too good to share." It was made by a local ad agency and signed off by the marketing department of Cadbury India – a department that Cadbury Schweppes admits contains no PR staff.

PR Week commented that the PR disaster inherent in selling chocolate through jokes about a conflict that has killed 50,000 people means it will not be long before Cadbury's forms a PR arm for its Indian operations.

Source: PR Week

CHAPTER 5

PR sectors and specialisms

Corporate PR

Many companies use Public Relations (PR) for marketing purposes. Typically such PR work is controlled by the marketing department or director and, as we have seen, is used alongside advertising and other promotional techniques. Corporate PR is distinct from this. It is typically run by a senior person, backed up by only a small team of helpers. Though seldom a member of the board of directors, he or she often reports directly to the chief executive and certainly has a lot of direct contact with the CEO and other senior staff. The term "PR" is normally dropped in favor of "Corporate Communications," "Corporate Affairs" or just "Communications." Their duties consist of managing the overall reputation of the company and its standing in the outside world. This is something that matters enormously to Chief Executives, who know that their jobs can be only one news story away from oblivion and that even the most powerful organizations are surprisingly vulnerable to hostile comment. CEOs themselves seldom have the skills, experience or confidence to deal with such difficulties on their own.

Business-to-business PR

Lower profile than consumer PR but very important, business-to-business (B2B) PR is about businesses communicating with other businesses – for example, component suppliers communicating with manufacturers, and manufacturers communicating with wholesalers and retailers. Much of this communication takes place within the specialist business press – such as trade magazines – although the business and specialist sections and pages of the national media can also be used.

Financial PR

Financial PR employs the most highly paid consultants in the business and can be hugely important, contributing to the making and breaking of companies. It is also one of the more secretive and least known PR specialisms.

Financial PR derives its importance from the decisive role a company's reputation plays in determining its share price. Media reports can quickly push the price up or down, with decisive consequences for the careers of senior executives. Typically the target audiences for financial PR are very limited: they are the small number of financial analysts and others who determine whether a company's shares are to be bought or sold. While PR always needs careful consideration when a company announces its financial results, it really comes to the fore at times of change or crisis: mergers, takeovers and corporate difficulties. The relevant media are specialist business publications, including international newspapers, such as the *Financial Times* and *Wall Street Journal*, and the business sections of the mainstream media (indeed many financial PR people are ex-financial journalists). To a much greater extent than most other forms of PR, financial PR is about playing down, within legal limits, news which companies do not wish to emerge. One way of achieving this is to employ large and powerful financial PR consultancies which have some bargaining power with the financial media.

Financial PR work is concentrated in the big financial marketplaces, such as London, Hong Kong, Mumbai and Singapore (the largest British financial specialist, Brunswick, is already established in Beijing and Hong Kong[1]). While in the first instance it can be undertaken in-house, the sheer volumes of PR work involved in major corporate battles, together with the need to bring in additional expertise and bargaining power, mean that financial PR consultancies tend to play a big part in many critical situations. In view of its importance to the smooth operation of the markets, financial PR has come to be more closely regulated than most other forms of PR work.

Consumer PR

Consumer PR is about helping to sell consumer goods: it is business to consumer communications, or B2C. As such it is very much a branch of marketing. Typically consumer PR campaigns (and their budgets) are controlled by companies' marketing directors. As described above, consumer PR is used alongside other marketing techniques, such as advertising and sales promotions. It can be undertaken in-house, but very often consultancies with a particular flair for consumer PR are brought in to run specific campaigns.

The first challenge for consumer PR people is – normally – to get any kind of media coverage at all for their client's product. Given the huge number of products in circulation in any modern economy, getting a particular product into the media represents a challenge which is compounded by the fact that most products are not intrinsically interesting from a news editor's point of view. Ingenuity is required in order to make the product newsworthy while ensuring that it gets the right kind of coverage and that the message is not overshadowed or undermined by the PR. Typically this involves some combination of overlapping ingredients such as celebrity endorsement, a publicity stunt, a photo opportunity, a competition, or interesting facts and figures on consumer lifestyles.

Using celebrities for consumer PR for Nike in China

Weber Shandwick, the international PR consultancy, works for Nike, including the Nike Pro account and the sports brand's basketball, football, women's sports and sports culture lines.

One focus of the campaign is upcoming China basketballer Yi Jian Lian.

Source: PR Week

At present consumer PR in many Asian markets is largely focused on staple products, but economic growth is bringing more heavily branded goods and more luxury items within reach of larger numbers of consumers. The marketing of such products often requires a combination of PR and advertising. A second arena for consumer PR is the international market. At present there are only a very limited number of global superbrands with Asian origins, but as the Indian and Chinese superbrands emerge their promotion will involve large amounts of PR.

Promoting Chinese beer

"I love getting PR packages. The latest one that I received within this past week is for Tsingtao, the lager from China – their number one beer, and in fact is the "Number 1 branded consumer product exporter from China." That's according to the press materials."

Thus commented an American beer enthusiast on his website where he regularly reviews different beers and lagers. He mentions that the marketing was focused on Chinese New Year, or the Year of the Pig, and he received in addition to the beer a T-shirt and a folder of background material.

In addition to conventional consumer goods, there are PR people using similar techniques for every kind of product and service. **Travel PR** helps to sell holidays and flights and accommodation for business trips, most typically by inviting journalists or well-known people to enjoy travel free of charge in the expectation that they will give the travel facilities favorable coverage, while other firms specialize in hotels and restaurants. **Fashion PR** is an important specialism in its own right. Other examples include **music and entertainment PR**. In all cases the PR work may be undertaken in-house or by consultancies. Indeed many of the bigger PR consultancies have set up specialist subsidiaries to tackle such business. This represents a recognition that the image and approach they offer their traditional corporate clients may not seem right for markets such as these.

Lobbying, public affairs, government relations and political consultancy

What is lobbying?

Lobbying can be defined as any action designed to influence the actions of government. This includes not just national legislatures or parliaments, but also central government ministries and agencies and the growing army of regulators; international organizations (such as the United Nations (UN), the International Monetary Fund (IMF), the World Bank and the World Trade Organization (WTO)); and regional and local tiers of government. In short there is potential for lobbying activity wherever political power is located and wherever decisions are made on laws and regulations and their implementation.

Clearly in this sense lobbying is timeless: all kinds of organizations in all societies have always had an interest in influencing governments. However the origins of the term are telling, deriving as they do from the lobby of a Washington hotel where businessmen and others sought to waylay the US President Grant in the late nineteenth century. Since then lobbying has become a large, specialized activity, employing tens of thousands of people in Washington alone. In Europe Brussels, as the center of the European Union's administration, has become a center for lobbying activity. Lobbying remains the term which most outsiders know and recognize. However, in a way which parallels the use of the term PR, many "lobbyists" prefer not to call themselves that, in view of lobbying's associations with secretive deals and even corruption. Instead such terms as "public affairs," "government affairs," "government relations" and "political consultancy" are often preferred (although confusingly these can mean slightly different things to different people). Beyond the business world charities and campaigning organizations such as Greenpeace and Amnesty International, which would never use the word "lobbying" to describe their activities, in practice do a great deal of it as they try to influence governments and international organizations.

In the United States and Europe lobbying gradually became a professionalized, specialist activity as the role of governments in society and the economy grew. However, the market liberalization which began in the 1980s and has since swept the world has given lobbying an enormous boost. Large parts of the economy which were in state hands are now privately owned and run: direct government control has ended, but government legislation and regulation have an enormous impact on the way in which businesses are run, and hence businesspeople want to influence such decisions. Increasingly popular anxieties about issues, be they to do with security, food, medical treatment, health and safety, environmental or other matters, are met by governments through legislation and regulation. Lobbying represents an opportunity for different voices to be heard before policy is decided, and for government it can be welcome, offering access to a range of expert information and views before decisions are made.

The work of lobbyists can be broken down as follows:

- First, and most minimally, to provide information and advance warning. In the modern world it is hard for any organization to keep up with the large amounts of legislation and regulation which might affect it (and which may, for example, have serious cost implications). Even if it is impossible to do anything to influence government, the more advance notice organizations have the more they are able to prepare themselves. Thus many organizations pay lobbyists to monitor the work of obscure arms of government, legislatures and international organizations – and indeed even some government organizations pay for such services in order to find out about what the rest of government is up to, so big and so complex has the work of government become.
- To amend proposed government measures, or even to stop them in their tracks or, if all else fails, overturn them. This is the classic focus of lobbying. Lobbyists always urge the need to get involved at the earliest stage in the policy-making process, before policy is settled. The earlier they are involved, the easier it is to change policy. However lobbying can continue up to and beyond the passage of legislation (there is, for example, often considerable leeway about the way new laws are implemented).
- Lobbying can also be used to urge government action.

Who lobbies?

Anyone can lobby, but the biggest users of lobbying are business (including business organizations), charities and other campaigning not-for-profit organizations. While the business world is firmly associated with lobbying in the public mind, not-for-profit organizations are often even more focused on it: many such organizations exist solely to campaign for a cause (whereas commercial organizations have their core businesses to attend to), and thus lobbying lies at the heart of what they do.

As with other forms of PR, lobbying can be undertaken "in-house," by lobbyists who are directly employed by the organization, or by an external firm – or by a combination of the two. Only relatively large organizations or ones which are particularly concerned about government action will normally deem it worthwhile to employ full-time lobbyists, but many businesses are members of trade organizations and one of the main functions of such bodies is to lobby on behalf of the common interests of their members. Some organizations will retain the services of lobbying firms to maintain a watching brief (see p. 24) and then use them for specific campaigns when the need arises.

Lobbying in Hong Kong: a PR trade body seeking to influence legislation which could impact on day-to-day PR work

In 2004 the Council of Public Relations Firms of Hong Kong wrote to the Hong Kong Government expressing serious concerns that forthcoming changes to intellectual property legislation would make the copying of media materials – something which PR people do routinely in the course of their work in order to monitor media coverage – illegal, and might make member firms subject to legal sanctions.

Source: www.cprfhk.org

Like PR people generally, lobbyists can come from a range of backgrounds: no specific qualifications are required. However, just as journalistic expertise is often valued in mainstream PR, political and governmental experience is often an entry ticket for the world of lobbying. In order to influence government, a proper understanding of the way it works is essential, and very often direct personal knowledge of key personalities is seen as advantageous.

The relationship between lobbying and the rest of the PR industry

Some lobbyists like to dissociate themselves from Public Relations, seeing media relations as a blunt instrument compared with their ability to target the real decision-makers in government. Many lobbying firms are independent, specialist businesses, which do not undertake general PR work, while other organizations – law firms, for example – may offer lobbying services. However, almost all large PR consultancies offer lobbying alongside other services and therefore employ specialist lobbyists: it is now part of what many of their clients expect, and lobbying campaigns may be combined with other forms of PR work in pursuit of common objectives. Lobbying work can be carried on discreetly and effectively, without other forms of PR activity, but if additional pressure is required, all political organizations pay great attention to media coverage, and so media relations and lobbying can go hand in hand.

Politics and PR

Political leaders have always been interested in their public images, and to that extent politicians have always practiced PR. However, the emergence of the modern media has both given politicians new means of communication and also left them vulnerable: political PR is very often about defending individuals, parties and policies from the media. At the same time the growth of new concepts of public accountability and the spread of democracy in many countries has created new reasons for politicians to hire PR talent, although interestingly the term "Public Relations" has disappeared from the political world in most English-speaking countries.

As a result of these trends political PR people – called spokespeople, press officers or communications experts – are not only more numerous than ever before, they also enjoy more power and status. Critics often see political PR as particularly manipulative and ruthless, and in many Western countries the nickname "spin" is used and the practitioners are called "spin doctors."

One difference between commercial and political PR is that the latter is much more often negative. In the world of business public attacks on competitors are relatively rare: they risk drawing attention to rivals and also threaten to drag the relevant business sector into disrepute. In democracies, on the other hand, negative campaigning and attacks on political opponents are commonplace. A second difference is that personalities are far more often at the heart of political PR activity: political leaders tend to have much higher profiles than business leaders and are constantly aware of how they are covered (or not covered) by the media.

Although political "spin" has attracted a lot of attention, and its influence has spread around much of the world, it blurs into another kind of political PR, one which is practiced in all societies. All governments need to communicate with their citizens, whether through existing mass media or directly (through, for example, leaflets, events or government websites). This may involve educating people about public health or crime prevention, informing them about new educational opportunities or even threatening them with dire consequences if they do not pay their taxes. Whatever the message, there is usually some scope for "spin" and such communication has become an increasingly important part of modern government, with more and more specialist staff being employed.

National governments also need to reach international audiences in order to foster goodwill and to promote specific objectives such as increased trade, investment, travel and tourism. This has led to an increase in what is called public diplomacy, whereby countries use PR alongside other promotional tools to seek to enhance their reputations.

"Spin doctors" have become part of party political life in India as political parties compete for votes. In 2004 spin doctors working for the BJP's leader, Mr Vajpayee, coined the slogan "India Shining," a reference to what they said was a feel-good factor sweeping the country, and a phrase which echoed Ronald Reagan's famous "Good Morning America." However many saw the slogan as misjudged, and out of keeping with the experiences of many ordinary Indians – perhaps a pointer to the sort of pitfalls which PR people who belong to an out-of-touch affluent, educated urban elite are apt to suffer. In the event the BJP lost the election.

The not-for-profit sector

Most people firmly associate PR with the world of business, and are also familiar with its use in politics (where it is often given the nickname of "spin" and is seen as the work of "spin doctors"). However, they are less familiar with its use by the third sector – not-for-profit organizations, non-governmental organizations (NGOs), charities and campaigning organizations. These are increasingly important and should not be overlooked by any PR person – even if, as we shall see, he or she wishes to remain in the business sector.

Although there have always been charities, and examples of campaigning organizations can be found throughout history, the number of such organizations has grown phenomenally in recent decades. According to one estimate, fewer than a thousand such organizations were operating internationally in the late 1950s, but today there are more than 44,000 of them. According to another estimate they employ nearly twenty million people (quite apart from huge amounts of volunteer time) and enjoy an annual income of well over $1,000 billion. Although many such organizations are small and obscure, they increasingly follow the pattern of the corporate sector, with powerful, well-known global superbrands such as Greenpeace, Friends of the Earth, the World Wildlife Fund (WWF), and Amnesty International.

Despite the growing importance of such organizations and the high profile nature of the campaigns they run they are seldom identified with PR. They almost never use the term to describe what they do and are almost never picked upon by critics of PR. In fact, of course, campaigning organizations such as the superbrands named above deploy enormous PR muscle, even if they call it campaigning or something else. Unlike commercial organizations which have to produce goods or deliver services, campaigning NGOs can concentrate all their energies on PR, including high-profile publicity stunts of a kind of which commercial PR people can only dream. This means that there are plenty of good career opportunities to be found in working for them. It also means that commercial and governmental PR people need to be well aware of the PR activities of NGOs as they are usually at the receiving end of their criticisms and, indeed, need to spend increasing proportions of their working lives dealing with them. There is a even a niche career path for seasoned NGO campaigners who then sell their skills and experience to private sector organizations which are being troubled by NGO activism.

NGOs start with an inbuilt PR advantage: trust. Repeated surveys show that in most countries they are more trusted than governments and the media – and often more trusted than business. This means that whatever they say is more likely to be believed and respected. This seems to be becoming more and more true in Asia. One recent survey of international opinion leaders by the international PR consultancy Edelman[2] found that in China while government was still the most trusted of these sectors (trusted by 78 percent), followed by business at 67 percent, trust in NGOs had risen dramatically in the past few years, from 31 percent in 2004 to 56 percent in 2007. While business is currently more trusted than NGOs in India, it is likely that Asian business and governments will increasingly experience problems at the hands of high-profile NGOs.

The commercial sector's PR responses to NGO campaigning have evolved in the face of this growing challenge. One response has been to set up and fund organizations which can research and debate contentious issues, such as climate change or pollution. If these organizations are at one remove from the companies themselves they can be seen as more independent and therefore more authoritative – and sometimes their views and research findings are reported in this way by the media. However opponents often deride such organizations as mere "front groups" for their corporate paymasters. Another common technique has been to engage in dialogue with NGOs and to make – or appear to make – limited concessions, thereby appeasing the NGO. This also helps pull the debate on to more moderate ground and away from extreme positions. Those opponents who remain can readily be depicted as an extremist minority and contrasted with moderate opponents.

Use of an eye-catching publicity stunt by Greenpeace India

To highlight the impact of burning coal for electricity production on the climate Greenpeace India beamed messages on to the cooling towers of the state owned Raichur Thermal Power Plant. This action comes close on the heels of a similar activity at the Ennore thermal power plant near Chennai, also in India. Greenpeace is using these publicity tactics to draw attention to what it sees as the devastating impacts of climate change in India and the shift to renewable energy that it believes the Government should implement to avert this disaster.

Source: Greenpeace India

Internal communications

As the clichés have it, today an organization's employees are its most important ambassadors and its greatest asset. Motivating and retaining key staff has moved center stage, and ways have to be found to get across the important messages associated with rapid change. This puts a premium on communication, and in large, dispersed organizations ordinary communication between managers and the people they manage is seldom enough. Instead internal communications has emerged as a discipline and describes the process of deliberate, planned communication within an organization which is undertaken by specialist staff. The means used can vary: while internal communications is most commonly associated with newsletters, it can extend to a full range of media – including intranets, internal TV and radio – as well as different kinds of meetings and staff activities, where it often merges with staff training.

Internal communications is sometimes controlled by human resources or personnel managers, but is an increasingly important part of the contemporary PR scene. Sometimes called employer branding, it is of particular importance in the burgeoning service sector, where companies no longer sell identical manufactured goods. When selling services every transaction is different and the behavior of the employee is crucial: one of the best-known examples is call centres, where the behavior of each individual staff member who talks to customers over the phone is of critical importance. Employer branding plays an important role in conditioning and standardizing such behavior. As the branding guru Wally Olins has put it:

> In order to get an effective service brand, people have to be taught to live the brand they work with. For the customer, the person who represents the brand is the brand.

Another commonly used term, change management, reflects the role of internal communications in guiding staff through periods of upheaval, including relocation, restructuring and redundancy.

CHAPTER 6

The reputation of Public Relations

Public Relations (PR) often says that it is the discipline that looks after reputation and that reputation matters a great deal. It seems only fair therefore briefly to consider PR's own reputation and its implications for the industry.

In popular culture – films, television and novels – Western PR people tend to be portrayed in two contrasting ways: as young, frivolous and almost always female – and working in marketing Public Relations (MPR); and as more senior, serious and sinister – spin doctors playing for big stakes in the world of politics or big corporations (and usually male). The former is better known and is associated with international television hits such as *Sex in the City* and *Absolutely Fabulous* as well as films such as *Sliding Doors* and *Bridget Jones' Diary*.

"Miss PR"

The first international PR firm only began work in China in 1984 (the year that the term "Public Relations" was first used in the official newspaper *Economic Daily*), so for many ordinary Chinese people their introduction to PR was the popular TV series "Miss PR," first shown in 1988. The series featured a group of young and pretty girls working as "Miss PR" in a hotel. This image of PR remained quite influential, with PR people often being associated with quite lowly roles such as receiving guests, although it was very much at odds with how international and domestic PR firms viewed their work.

Source: Yujie He's University of Westminster MA thesis

Some of these stereotypes can also be found in the news media in developed countries, where the portrayal is often actively hostile. Since its beginnings, PR has frequently been disparaged in the press. Fairly or unfairly, journalists have portrayed PR people as, alternatively, people who plague them with stories that they do not want to cover or as people who block their way when there is a story which they *do* want to cover. In pursuit of these goals PR people are credited with using all kinds of tricks, something that journalists claim to resent. It may be early days for PR in much of Asia in this regard, but some tension between the worlds of journalism and PR is inevitable and in our view healthy.

Like any successful satire these portrayals of PR, however superficial, must have some grounding in truth. The PR industry worries about them and sees them as negative but in reality they have had little impact on the growth of the industry. However it is depicted in the media and popular culture, plenty of people are eager to work in the industry, more and more PR courses have been developed, senior managers of large organizations seem anxious to hire more PR people, and overall the industry has enjoyed faster growth than the economy. It seems that some of the characteristics of PR displayed in these films and TV programs actually attract people: for many, a well-paid, varied job in a big city seems alluring, while others like the idea of pulling strings behind the scene. For those who employ PR people the fact that they annoy journalists may be perfectly all right – the aim of PR is not to please journalists. Moreover, a detached observer would note that PR people are normally better paid than journalists and enjoy better working conditions and career prospects: journalistic bitterness is sometimes more than tinged with envy, and whatever they say many journalists choose to become PR people.

However, these portrayals of PR do have some practical consequences. First, they are one of the main reasons why so many PR people have dropped the term "Public Relations" to describe what they do. They hope that by giving themselves different job titles they will avoid the stigma they see as attached to PR. Second, it can affect the standing of PR within the workplace, with PR people at risk of being seen as relatively unimportant, and even undermine the industry's own self-confidence. Third, they have had an impact on the official organs of the PR industry. PR organizations pour a great deal of effort into trying to portray PR as a serious, ethical profession. The emphasis on codes of conduct and on PR education is in part a response to the depictions described above.

How people see PR in Vietnam

According to Mya chairman Tuan Anh Phan, an internal study conducted among 30 PR firms in 2007 exposed a lack of understanding of strategic PR in the country.

Chief among findings was that 71 percent "strongly disagreed" that strategic planning had a place in PR, while 62 percent believed PR only meant generating publicity.

Source: PR Week

CHAPTER 7

The Law and Public Relations

It is true to say that Public Relations (PR) practitioners are not normally as preoccupied with legal matters as journalists. Whereas the media provides information and comment about many people and organizations, all of which may take umbrage at what is reported, PR people are for the most part seeking to put across positive information with the full authority of the organizations for which they work – a less risky activity. Similarly mainstream business activity has legally enforceable contracts at its heart, as people seek to buy and sell goods and services, whereas in media relations work the relationship between PR person and journalist is much more informal and seldom seen as a legal matter. Nonetheless, PR people must avoid slipping into complacency. Their day-to-day work involves making highly public statements on behalf of the organizations for which they work, and saying things which can have potentially serious implications. They are still very much subject to the law and can fall foul of it, with embarrassing and costly results for them and those who employ them.

This section does not attempt to provide definitive advice – that should be sought from lawyers – nor can it seek to cover the ramifications of the many different legal systems in Asia. PR people are all subject to the law of the land where they work, and increasingly need to consider legal systems in other countries and international law as well (for example, it will not be enough for those seeking to export Asian brands to worldwide markets to satisfy themselves that they are complying with domestic law). Some aspects of the law impinging on PR are ones that concern everyone working in business. For example, those running PR consultancies are also businesspeople in their own right and need to be conversant with the key principles of commercial law and employment legislation. In-house PR employees may find themselves putting in place many legally binding contracts with suppliers as they set up PR campaigns.

In addition, particular branches of PR have their own legal preoccupations. Financial PR people have to be particularly careful about what they say because of the growing body of law governing the financial markets. Similar concerns affect healthcare PR in some countries, while lobbyists increasingly find themselves subject to laws designed to stamp out corruption. However, we have focused on those aspects of the law which are most specific to PR overall: you may not be a lawyer, but you need to know when to stop what you are doing and get expert advice before you proceed. Remember that you are also likely to be your employer's first port of call if they feel their legal rights are being threatened in the media – the law is there for you as well, and there may be times when you need to take legal action (or at least threaten to do so). Finally, bear in mind that the law and its interpretation are constantly changing: keep an eye out for developments which might affect you.

Intellectual property

Every PR person needs at least a passing knowledge of intellectual property legislation as it is fundamental to branding and corporate identity and hence touches on so much of what they do. Intellectual property law operates both nationally and, increasingly, internationally. It is a double-edged sword: you may be at risk of infringing someone else's rights, but similarly you may need to protect your own. A useful source of further information is the World Intellectual Property Organization – www.wipo.int. The two main forms of intellectual property are **copyright** and **industrial property**.

Copyright, which is often referred to as author's rights, gives protection to many common forms of expression such as books, articles, speeches, music, paintings, photos, films and computer programs and databases. This means that you have to be very careful about using the work of other people in your PR campaigns and other activities, as you may well need prior permission and have to pay the copyright holder (the author, or whoever ownership has passed to). Although, there are some exemptions – for example, allowing brief quotations in certain contexts – there is a risk otherwise that you could be sued for infringing the owner's copyright. In most countries copyright is conferred automatically: there may be no particular sign to indicate that material you find in the media, for example, is copyright, but it remains protected. Nor can you assume that the work you commission for a PR campaign belongs to you: unless the contract states otherwise, copyright remains with the author. Thus, for example, if you commission a photographer to take photographs for a particular brochure and then decide to make further use of them you must ensure this is covered in your contract with the photographer or reach a separate agreement. By the same token your own organization's work is also protected by copyright and you can take steps to defend it.

It is important to note that copyright protection only extends to the actual form of expression – the words, images, sounds and so on – not the ideas on which they are based. However using other people's ideas may create other legal problems (see below) and, even if not illegal, the practice can cause embarrassment if it is exposed.

Industrial property includes, among other things, trademarks; commercial names and designations; inventions or patents – new solutions to technical problems; and industrial designs.

Trade marks – the logos, or words, symbols and images which are now inseparable from many familiar products – and commercial names and designations are fundamental to brand management and are fiercely protected by companies. Any attempt to use someone else's trade mark or commercial name could leave you facing legal action, and even using anything similar to an existing trade mark or name could be deemed an infringement: again, the rule is that if you are in any doubt you should seek expert advice.

While the other forms of industrial property seem less immediately relevant to PR, there have been attempts to patent ways of doing business. If these apply – or in the future come to apply-to you – they could have important implications for PR, not least because many consultancies claim to have developed distinctive ways of running PR programs. The position on the protection of computer programs also varies, and so PR people need to think carefully about the implications of using these.

Defamation

Most PR is about promoting organizations and their products and services, but sometimes PR work involves attacking competitors and rivals. In such circumstances PR people need to remember that they are just as much subject to the laws of defamation – libel and slander – as anyone else, whatever form of expression is used (be it a press release, a phone conversation or something posted on a website). Defamation cases can be long-drawn out, high profile and potentially very embarrassing and costly. Although the position on defamation will vary greatly between different countries' jurisdictions, in general any criticisms must either be seen as fair comment – a reasonable opinion that anyone might form – and/or based on hard evidence.

If your organization considers suing for defamation itself, you will obviously need good legal advice, but you will also need to consider very carefully the PR implications for your organization. Even if legal victory seems to be guaranteed, is a long-drawn out court case in which lots of potentially embarrassing evidence emerges, and in which senior company officials who are not used to the spotlight of publicity face cross-examination, going to be in your organization's best interests? What about the cost in terms of management time and resources? If you are taking on a small media outlet or group of activists will your organization be seen as acting like a heavy handed bully? When the global fast-food giant McDonald's took legal action against two activists who had been leafleting its braches in London they won a victory in the courts but were generally seen as suffering a major PR reverse.

Other aspects of the law

PR people have been affected by international moves towards, on the one hand, freedom of information legislation and, on the other, data protection laws. The former can mean that they are forced to reveal stored information: in the United Kingdom, for example, the government faced some embarrassment when it was obliged to reveal comments media relations staff had made about well-known journalists. Data protection laws on the other hand mean that PR people have to be evermore careful about what they say publicly about customers and others associated with their organizations. The privacy legislation which is emerging in some jurisdictions and which seeks to protect individuals' private lives from media intrusion can have similar implications, but more usually it is something PR people consider using to protect individuals working for their organizations from media attention.

Potential legal issues which can arise when corporations make public statements

In the USA Nike, the world's largest maker of sports shoes, was accused of making false statements about its use of labor in Asia to manufacture sportswear. Activists claimed that the workforce was forced to work in sweatshop conditions and that American consumers were deceived.

Nike has sought to "fight to preserve the right to free and open debate ... Companies should be free to voice their opinions through PR or advertising on major issues that impact their business."

Nike claimed that the US Constitution's protection of free speech guarantees the right to make their statements when they are about a social issue, rather than the product itself. Claims about the product are regarded as commercial speech which is regulated.

In the end Nike agreed to pay $1.5 million to the Fair Labor Association to settle the case.

The case was closely watched and widely seen as a test of corporate free speech.

Source: www.bbc.co.uk

CHAPTER 8

Public Relations ethics

Public Relations (PR) ethics are a much-discussed subject and are often in the media spotlight. Indeed allegations of unethical practice are one of the reasons that some practitioners have chosen to abandon using the term "Public Relations" to describe what they do. Most national and international PR organizations have produced ethical codes which they require members to uphold, and PR ethics features on most university courses for would-be practitioners. However what is – and is not – considered ethical behavior varies. All PR people are subject to the law, but beyond that what is considered acceptable social or business practice will depend on the prevailing culture. The considerations are not just a matter of morality: there are many perfectly legal things which PR people might do which could make them and the organization they serve very unpopular and lower their standing in the eyes of others. This section looks at some of the common ethical issues and how PR practitioners can approach them.

The codes of practice adopted by different PR organizations may vary, but they also have many common features. The codes of the International Public Relations Association (IPRA) share the key principles of individual countries' codes,[1] and they have been used here as a basis for discussing some specific ethical concerns. What follows is a paraphrase of IPRA's Code of Venice (called after where it was agreed), with a commentary on the implications of each item in the Code. The Code overlaps in many ways with IPRA's other, shorter, general code, the Code of Athens.

"In India, the power of PR has yet to gain true recognition. With more than 1,000 PR agencies in the country, the PRCAI gives all of us the opportunity to rally around and collaborate on common issues and priorities facing us. We are committed to defining the 'gold standards' in critical areas such as professional practices, professional standards, talent and delivery."

Ajay Kakar, President of the Public Relations Consultants Association of India (PRCAI)

Source: PR Week

- A general duty of fair dealing towards clients and employers, past and present.
  This seems straightforward and unexceptional, but of course the difficulty lies in deciding what constitutes "fair dealing": this can be quite flexible, and there is always a danger of interpreting the term in a self-serving way. It is usually a mistake to flout the accepted rules of the business community so a knowledge of generally accepted practice in the circumstances, together with reliance on one's individual conscience, is crucial.
- Not representing conflicting or competing interests without their consent.
  This generally accepted principle is shared with the advertising industry. It is clearly difficult for a single agency to do its utmost for two rivals, and there would be a serious risk of commercially sensitive information passing into rival hands. Historically both PR consultancies and advertising agencies have resigned lucrative accounts in order to take on even more lucrative business for rivals. Indeed one reason the big international marketing services groups such as WPP or Interpublic include more than one PR consultancy and more than one advertising agency is so that they can thus serve competing businesses. Since it is hard to hide the identity of clients (and declaring a client list is often a requirement) this principle is generally adhered to. The main problem applies if the conflict is not obvious or the competition is indirect: here commonsense and a sense of judgment are required.
- Safeguarding confidences of clients and employers.
  This notion of confidentiality is an important feature of most professional codes and goes well beyond PR – it represents what is expected of

doctors or lawyers for example. Clearly PR people cannot expect clients or employers to talk to them frankly unless they know their confidence will be respected. The main issue which might arise here is if there are legal or regulatory reasons to reveal what a client or employer is planning or doing – or if the PR practitioner feels that there are public interest issues (see below).

- Not attacking other organizations.

  It might seem nicer never to attack others and only to say positive things about oneself, and often it makes good practical sense as well: big organizations and major brands don't necessarily want to appear negative or draw attention to rivals. However some forms of PR would almost collapse if this rule was applied: NGOs such as Greenpeace put much of their effort into attacking major corporates and governments, and much – some would say most – political PR is negative. Some would also see a ban on negative PR in the commercial world as anticompetitive: within the law there is nothing wrong with attacking a rival as it allows consumers more information on which to make informed choices. Attacking poor products and poor service could serve the consumer's – and hence the public's – interest. One practical problem with applying this principle is that attacks on rivals can be indirect – they are often not actually named.

- In performing services for a client or employer, fees (or the equivalent, including gifts) should only be accepted from the client or employer (i.e. not from any third party), unless the client agrees otherwise.

  While this is not normally a problem, clearly there would be a possibility of conflict of interest if one was being paid from more than one source for the same work.

- Payment by results should neither be proposed nor accepted.

  This does not feature in all PR codes. It is partly driven by a desire to be comparable to other professions, where the client accepts that the professional applies their skills as best they can but payment is due regardless of the outcome. Thus doctors are paid even if patients do not recover, and lawyers were traditionally paid irrespective of the outcome of the case (this is changing with the advent of no-win no-fee agreements). However, some business people like to link payments to PR people to actual achievements, and in a competitive market some PR people are prepared to accept this rather than forego the business. Aside from the issue of whether it undermines PR's claim to professional standing, the main problem is determining the degree to which PR is responsible for any outcome. Marketing PR, for example, is very commonly used in conjunction with advertising and sales promotions and so singling out the achievement of PR is difficult and tends to be a matter of judgment. In crisis management, despite the best efforts of PR people the situation may still be bad for the organization concerned, but PR may have improved things: how is that relative success to be measured? Similarly, it would be tempting but untrue for PR people to take the credit for every success story.

- Conducting professional activities with respect to the public interest and individual dignity.

  Many PR codes contain a general statement of this kind, but of course defining what is meant by the public interest is fraught with difficulty and will always tend to come down to individual conscience. The Public Relations Society of America[2], for instance, defines "public interest" as conforming to the US Constitution but this is rather stating the obvious: all PR people are subject to the law. Giving priority to the public interest could clash with those areas of the code (see above) which emphasize duties to the client or employer. At the very least a PR person who felt that the public interest was threatened might have to resign the account or leave their job. In practice, few PR people enjoy the luxury of never disagreeing with those paying them, but, equally, few continue working for people with whom they are completely at odds.

- Not engaging in practices which tend to corrupt the integrity of public communication.

  Making payments or gifts to journalists or others in the media is a taboo area for PR in many countries. Journalists often pride themselves on their independence and objectivity, and PR people pride themselves on their ability to secure the right kind of coverage without money changing hands. However, without paying journalists anything PR people can offer them exclusive stories, and these are valuable in their own right as they can lead to promotion and salary increases for the journalists involved. Similarly, PR people can offer free holidays – the staple of travel PR – and other valuable and sought-after perks – and these have become essential prerequisites of modern media production.

- Not deliberately telling lies.

  This might seem simple and uncontroversial at first glance, and is not just an ethical matter as passing on untrustworthy information can be counterproductive. If it comes to be known that a PR person is not a source of reliable information then journalists and others will look elsewhere for their information. Therefore telling lies about specific facts and

figures is usually a bad idea, and in some contexts may be illegal. Beyond that social attitudes to lying vary. No one – including journalists – expects PR people to tell the full truth about the organizations they serve. Real disputes, disunity and problems will frequently have to be glossed over or even denied, but such lying is normally considered socially acceptable. Indeed a PR person who sought to tell the full truth in such situations would probably find himself or herself without a job. The issue continues to be hotly disputed. For example in 2007, following a large debate in London sponsored by the trade magazine PR Week a majority of the audience – made up of PR practitioners and students – voted by a small majority that PR people did not have a duty to tell the truth.

- Giving a faithful representation of the organization which the PR person serves.
  This overlaps with the point on lying above. The organization is paying for the service so no one will be surprised that the PR person accentuates the positive and minimizes the negative aspects of it in portraying it to journalists and others. A truly faithful representation would have to include detailing all an organization's faults!

- Not creating or using organizations which serve the undisclosed special interests of the organization the PR person serves.
  Businesses often have important interests in public debates which can affect their ability to carry on or develop their business activities. This might include their ability to build new plants, environmental controls, or their ability to promote and sell their products (the tobacco industry has faced particular problems in this regard). They have long realized that their voice in such debates will be undermined if they are simply seen to be furthering their commercial interests. To counter this, many business organizations have set up or contribute towards what are called "front groups" – business-sponsored lobbying groups which disguise (or certainly do not publicize) their business links.

- Not injuring the professional reputation or practice of other PR practitioners.
  This is clearly intended to stop unseemly attempts to undermine rivals in a way which would run counter to the behavior expected of a proper profession and could damage the standing of the PR industry. Of course attacks on business rivals can circumvent this by being subtle: other people's ways of doing business can be belittled without naming the practitioners. It might also be argued that this part of the code is anticompetitive and clashes with the injunction to respect the public

interest: what if a PR practitioner felt that he or she could offer a better service, or that the work of another was not in the public interest, and that the sanctions offered by the PR industry itself were inadequate?

- Not seeking to supplant other PR practitioners in their work by poaching their clients or their jobs.
  Again, this has a lot to do with PR's desire for professional status – making it more akin to medicine or law than commerce. Most PR people would avoid doing this in too obvious a way, but, as suggested above, the supplanting of rivals can be achieved in subtle ways which are hard to stop. It could also be argued that this restriction is also anticompetitive and thus not in the public interest – that it is in the interests of users of PR for them to be fully aware of the range of options available to them and that it is then up to them to choose.

- Co-operating with other practitioners to uphold the ethical code.
  As we shall see, upholding and enforcing codes of PR ethics has proved to be very difficult, and PR practitioners are not generally keen on launching public attacks on their rivals.

Problems of enforcement

As mentioned, there are many codes of PR ethics and they are occasionally revised and added to. Indeed individual PR practitioners may be bound by more than one if they are members of both national and international PR bodies. However, they have proved very difficult to enforce. There are various reasons for this.

Membership of PR organizations in most countries is voluntary: in most societies anyone is free to practice PR (although whether they will succeed is quite another matter). This is likely to remain the case, and is arguably a positive characteristic of the PR industry which, as a result, has been able to grow and adapt itself very quickly, absorbing talented individuals from a wide range of backgrounds. Attempts at statutory regulation would not only be restrictive but would also be very difficult to implement. What exactly would be regulated? There is no generally accepted definition of PR, and those that are in widest circulation are very general (for example, saying PR is about reputation management) and hence would not be of much value to a regulator. Moreover the duties of PR people can overlap with those of other communication and management disciplines.

In practice there are two main ways which can be used to restrict entry to a profession. Often some combination of them is used. First, people can be denied the right to use the profession's name and job titles to describe what they do – just as an ordinary person cannot set up a lawyer's office or a doctor's surgery. In theory this works quite well as offenders can usually be spotted quite quickly and dealt with. The difficulty with applying this to PR is that many – and perhaps a growing number – of PR people actually prefer to use other job titles and descriptions: for them being forced to drop references to PR would not be a problem.

Second, certain duties can be specified as tasks which only members of the profession can perform. For example, only a doctor can prescribe certain drugs, or only a lawyer may have the right to appear in a court of law. It is very hard to know which exact duties could be reserved for PR people. Offering advice on reputation management is far too general – it is something all kinds of people are involved in. Even those specific tasks most closely associated with PR are often undertaken by others – we all may speak to journalists, on our own behalves, or on behalf of friends or the organizations for which we work. Saying that only PR people can contact, or be contacted by, the media would certainly not be acceptable to journalists, would be all but impossible to enforce and would indeed flout most ideas about individual freedom.

All of this means that membership of professional organizations is likely to remain optional for PR practitioners (or that, if attempts are made to make it compulsory, it will prove impractical and unworkable). This means that such organizations have only limited power – members are free to leave and carry on their business as before. This is one of the reasons why the codes of ethics are very rarely enforced, and on the rare occasions that they have been, the sanctions are usually quite slight. Indeed the world's largest PR organization, the Public Relations Society of America[3], states on its website that "emphasis on enforcement of the code has been eliminated."

Another major reason why it is hard to enforce PR's codes of ethics is that so much of the most critical PR work takes place behind the scenes, and involves private conversations and meetings. This makes it difficult to prove beyond doubt that someone has breached the ethical code. In contrast it is very rare for the more public face of PR – press releases and press conferences – to be called into question on ethical grounds. Instead PR's scandals often revolve around PR people's conversations being tape-recorded without their knowledge (or their failure to realize that email, although a very useful means of communication, leaves a permanent record). Thus in Britain the Queen's daughter-in-law, Sophie Wessex, who ran a PR consultancy, was forced to step down after an embarrassing conversation with a newspaper journalist posing as a potential client was tape-recorded and published (and, for the same reason, her business partner became a rare example of someone who was forced to leave the UK's Institute of Public Relations).

A final word on PR ethics

PR people suffer a permanent handicap: most of what is broadcast and printed about them is said and written by journalists, who in one sense are professional adversaries and in another sense are perhaps a little bitter about the fact that their "adversaries" enjoy better job prospects and salaries. As the people who ultimately produce media content, journalists have the last word. Certainly PR people can be convenient scapegoats in the public debate. We suspect that PR people are just as ethical as other people in business, government or indeed the not-for-profit sector. That means that mistakes are made and on occasion people act unethically, but by and large most people are aware of what is considered acceptable behavior, although as our commentary has indicated this is often rather more nuanced than these codes make it appear. They are also aware that it is seldom in their interests to be regarded as, or even suspected of being, unethical practitioners. PR people need to be fully aware of the ethical codes to which they and their organization have signed up but, on the other hand, being sanctimonious about PR work can be counterproductive: ordinary people have a pretty shrewd idea about PR and who pays for it and would not respect you if you pretend otherwise.

CHAPTER 9

The academic study of Public Relations

More and more academic courses in Public Relations (PR), at both undergraduate and postgraduate levels, are emerging around the world. Such courses first got underway in the United States in the early decades of the twentieth century and were being offered in Europe, particularly in Britain, by the late twentieth century. This trend is a tribute to the popularity of PR as a career, and indeed an ever-growing number of those starting out in PR now have degrees in the subject.

Despite this many senior figures in the PR industry remain skeptical about the value of PR education – as opposed to practical experience. PR education is a relatively recent phenomenon, and for the time being it remains the case that leading figures in the industry have themselves studied other subjects and, understandably, feel that they are at least as good a preparation for a career in PR. Moreover, PR will always be open to late entrants from other disciplines – especially journalism – who, by definition, are unlikely to have studied PR.

A wider issue is how far PR can be taught as an academic subject. Certainly some key skills can be taught in the classroom, and practiced by students in written work and through oral presentations and discussions. But much PR work depends on its social context: PR campaigns only really take shape through the interplay with journalists and others which leads, the PR person hopes, to the creation of the right kind of publicity. This will always be very difficult to simulate in the classroom: here education is definitely a second-best to practical experience.

Another problem is that many leading universities have been reluctant to offer degrees in PR. One reason for that is that too many

PR textbooks – not we hope this one! – have sought to prop up the reputation of PR rather than seeking after the truth in a traditional academic way. As a result they carry little weight, and are little known outside the limited field of academic PR. This is true for the some of the most influential concepts in academic PR, the four models first described by Grunig and Hunt in 1984.

These models, which have since been refined, show PR adopting the following four forms: *propaganda*; *public information*; *two-way asymmetric*; and *two-way symmetric*.

- The first of these, *propaganda*, is depicted as the most primitive form of PR, displaying relative indifference towards the truth. It is used in sports, theatre and in product promotion. In Grunig and Hunt's view, it accounts for 15 percent of the PR practice.
- In the case of the second, *public information*, used by governments, not-for-profit organizations and businesses, truth is important. It accounts for 50 percent of PR practice.
- *Two-way asymmetric* communication, used by competitive businesses, uses feedback to achieve "scientific persuasion," but although the communication is two-way the effect is imbalanced: the feedback is used simply to enhance the delivery of the message. It accounts for 20 percent of PR practice.
- Finally, *two-way symmetric* communication seeks to achieve "mutual understanding." Its two-way communication has balanced effects. It is used by professional leaders and accounts for 15 percent of PR practice.

However, Grunig and Hunt offer little evidence for the percentages of PR practice which they allocate to each category, nor do they convincingly show that anyone has really carried on PR with completely balanced effects in mind: after all the PR person is being paid by one party and so by definition is imbalanced. In practice these models, which feature in many PR textbooks, seem to be really about PR trying to draw a veil over its past and position itself as a more enlightened industry. Whether creating elaborate models which bear little relation to reality is a good way of achieving that is another matter.

One PR trade body's role in promoting education and training

As one of the longer established PR trade bodies in Asia, the Institute of Public Relations of Singapore has been concerned with educating both existing practitioners and those who want to work in PR since 1971. It currently offers:

A Professional Certificate in Public Relations and Mass Communication
A Diploma in Public Relations and Mass Communication
A Graduate Diploma in Marketing Communications
A Bachelor of Communication (Mass Communication)

Source: www.iprs.org.sg

PART II

Strategy and Planning

> "Beijing's bid for the Olympic Games has benefited a lot from Public Relations. We put special emphasis on Public Relations in every step during the bidding."
>
> Liu Jingmin, Vice-Mayor of Beijing

One of the biggest differences between Public Relations (PR) and journalism is that generally journalism is a very short-term business. At the end of the working day or week the journalist clears their desk and starts on a new story. Seldom does a journalist work on a story for more than a week or so. The exception to this rule is the specialist or investigative journalist. They may take months or even years building up their knowledge about a particular area of activity, but both are relatively rare creatures. Broadly, journalists work to very short planning cycles. Yesterday's news is just that. Once an issue is out or a program finished the journalist is on to the next edition or broadcast with little or no time to look back and reflect. The same is not true for a PR practitioner.

PR practitioners must plan a long way in advance. The situation or market of the organization they represent must be assessed. The overall objectives of that organization have to be understood and communication objectives devised and agreed that support those objectives. A strategic plan detailing how the objectives are going to be achieved, what tactics are to be used and how they are to be evaluated needs to be drawn up. This strategic plan then needs to be costed and presented to those that hold the purse strings in order to get their agreement.

There is an old saying that 'The Golden Rule is that those who hold the gold make the rules.' Without money and the backing of those at the top of an organization no PR plan can hope to succeed, and the most brilliant PR plan will be fruitless if you cannot persuade senior management of its wisdom. Moreover, even when the funding has been secured and the go-ahead given by the top there are still other internal groups who need to be persuaded. Few PR plans exist in a vacuum: other parts of the organization need to be on side and singing from the same song sheet. There is little point, for example, in securing excellent press coverage for a new initiative if the resultant stakeholder or customer interest is met with ignorance or even antipathy by employees or departments who have not been got on side at an early stage in the planning. In practice, therefore, a certain amount of diplomacy, persuasion and compromise is an inescapable part of the planning process.

Clearly planning is important, but how do you devise a PR plan? What is the difference between a business objective and a PR objective? How is strategy different from objectives? How can you persuade the people who hold the purse strings to support your plan? How do you know if your plan worked?

CHAPTER 10

POSTAR, a PR planning aid

In this section we explain the POSTAR planning model[1]. Not all of POSTAR will be relevant to all people all of the time, but it provides a clear and practical framework to formulate a Public Relations (PR) plan. It is not meant to be a straightjacket but an aid. Think of it as scaffolding. Depending on the size and shape of the "building," the more or less you will need to focus on the different elements of the POSTAR plan.

A major international organization may have an overall communications or PR plan made up of a number of POSTARs, with one each for consumer, financial, political, internal and even local community audiences. A small local firm may just have a basic consumer plan, but all organizations need a plan because relations with your publics are something you have whether you like it or not, in the same way that no business can exist without some sort of financial plan. As we have seen, organizations from time immemorial have practiced PR unconsciously, but the new challenge for Asia is to go about it in a planned and deliberate way, to your maximum advantage.

So what does POSTAR stand for?
POSTAR

POSITIONING
Where are we starting from?

OBJECTIVES
Where do we want to be?

STRATEGY
How are we going to get there? (Overall plan)

TACTICS
How are we going to get there? (Creative ideas)

ADMINISTRATION
What time and resources do we need/have to get there?

RESULTS
How will we know when we are there?

So in essence POSTAR determines where we are, where we want to be, how we are going to get there and how we will know when we are there. What could be simpler? Unfortunately the devil is in the detail.

Let us look at each of the stages more closely.

Positioning

A background or situation analysis can be broken down in to two distinct parts. The first part looks at the organization itself and may be described as the *internal analysis*, although it includes an analysis of the market in which the organization operates, its customers or clients and the competition. The second part looks at all the outside influences on the organization and can be described as the *external analysis* and includes political, legal and even environmental factors that may influence the success of your organization and your PR plan. Let us look first at the *internal analysis*.

Internal analysis

The internal analysis entails examining three separate groups:

- The organization
- The market
- The customers

The first thing to look at is *the organization* you are working for. It is amazing and a little depressing how many PR people forget this basic need.

What sort of organization is it? Who owns it? Is it big or small? Is it conservative or radical? Is it well funded or comparatively impoverished (lofty ideals always have to be tempered with reality)? And, most importantly, what are the overall objectives of the organization? If you do not know what the *organizational objectives* are you cannot devise a relevant PR plan. A useful analogy might be a country at war.

For example, the head of government of a country will determine whether to go to war or not and what the objectives of that war should be. This is equivalent to the CEO or leader of an organization deciding its overall objectives.

The head of government in consultation with his most senior generals will then decide what the best strategy and overall tactics are for achieving the stated objectives (see Table 10.1).

Responsibility cascades down. In effect the head of government's strategy becomes the generals' military objectives and the tactics *their* strategy. The Generals must now determine the best, detailed tactics to achieve the objectives and strategy. This is equivalent to the corporate affairs or communications director devising a plan to achieve the objectives set by the CEO.

The Generals now have to define the objectives for the commanders in the field. This is the equivalent to the communications director (or similar) briefing his PR team.

Table 10.1 shows how the objectives, strategy and tactics hierarchy might work in a war. Now try and apply it to your own organization using Table 10.2.

Once you clearly understand your organization's objectives and where you sit in the organizational hierarchy you can start to analyze the other aspects of your situational plan. To continue the military analogy, you can now look at the disposition of the enemy forces, how big or small they are in comparison to your own, and how the layout of the land may affect your plans.

The next area to look at is *the market*. Most of this data should be available from your marketing or commercial department. Market data is particularly important if you are involved in marketing PR. The sort of questions that need to be asked here are:

- What is the size and growth potential of the market ... or is it in decline and, if so, why?
- What are the trends in the market? For example, is there a move away from conventional retail and towards online sales?
- How is the economy performing now and what is predicted for the future?

Table 10.1

An example of objectives, strategy and tactics hierarchy

	Politicians	Senior Generals	Officers at the front
OBJECTIVES	Remove the enemy's ability to attack you	Employ superior air power to destroy transport and military infrastructure. Then defeat enemy in fast moving land war	Use high altitude bombers and cruise missiles to destroy infrastructure. Then employ tanks and paratroops in surprise attack
STRATEGY	Employ superior air power to destroy transport and military infrastructure. Then defeat enemy in fast moving land war	Use high altitude bombers and cruise missiles to destroy infrastructure. Then employ tanks and paratroops in surprise attack·	Use squadron 16 stealth bombers in 12 sorties over 2 weeks. Use 3 tank battalions to rush river positions at end of two week bombing
TACTICS	Use high altitude bombers and cruise missiles to destroy infrastructure. Then employ tanks and paratroops in surprise attack	Use squadron 16 stealth bombers in 12 sorties over 2 weeks. Use 3 tank battalions to rush river positions at end of two week bombing	Bombers to work at night in groups of 6. Tanks to go in at dawn in a sweeping motion

Table 10.2

Your objectives, strategy and tactics hierarchy			
	CEO	Communications Director	Public Relations Officers
OBJECTIVES			
STRATEGY			
TACTICS			

- What is the competition like and what are they doing? Are they aggressive or defensive? What sort of PR space do they occupy?

Inextricably linked with your analysis of the market is an analysis of *your customers*. If your customers are consumers, as opposed to other businesses or organizations, you need to ask questions such as:

- What age ranges do they cover? (Clearly, targeting young people will involve different media and tactics compared with targeting older people)
- What social class are they drawn from? For example, there would be little point in devising a strategy with heavy use of electronic media if they have little access to such media.
- What attitudes and cultural values do they share? An approach that may be right for a sophisticated and liberal urban customer

group could badly backfire with more conservative rural-based communities.

- Where do they live, and what are their shopping/buying traditions and patterns?

It is all too easy for well educated and comparatively affluent PR people living and working in major urban areas to become out of touch with less privileged groups in society. By the same token it can be hard for PR people fully to understand some of the needs and preoccupations of the super rich. As with so much in business, the answer is planning and analysis. As a military leader once said: "Fail to plan and you should plan to fail."

One of the potential strengths of local PR firms and in-house operations in Asia is their ability to understand local culture and their skill at communicating with the media and government. International PR firms have to try harder to compete.

If your customers are other organizations – for example, Business to Business (B2B) PR – you need to be asking questions such as:

- Who owns and controls them?
- What are their traditional buying patterns and are these likely to change? Who are the actual buyers, who the recommenders and who the 'rubber stampers'?
- Are these organizations tending to get larger and consolidate or are there a lot of new dynamic young players emerging?
- What are the issues affecting these organizations? (See the SLEPT analysis below)

So having analyzed the organization, market and customers you now need to think of the other groups who may impact on the success or failure of your organization.

External analysis

There are two stages to the external analysis. The first is the *stakeholder analysis* which looks at those who need to be influenced and those who influence the organization. This is also sometimes called

Figure 10.1

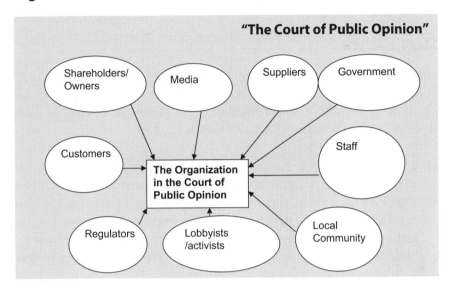

examining *the court of public opinion*. The second stage is what is called a SLEPT analysis and involves examining the external factors and issues that may impact on the organization and its stakeholders. First of all we need to look at the stakeholders or "court of public opinion."

Stakeholder analysis

Figure 10.1 is an example of a **stakeholder map**. Different stakeholders will apply to different organizations, but what is certain is that no organization can function effectively in PR terms unless it has drawn up a stakeholder map. It is also worth noting that 'staff' are included in this external planning phase when staff are really an internal audience. The justification for this is that staff are not only an organizational asset but also an audience who need to be communicated with not just in commercial terms but also in broader terms as a group who will have strong opinions on what the organization says and does. For example, if your organization is a food producer it has to be sensitive to different attitudes towards animals such as cows and pigs in different societies. These religious and cultural views will affect staff and their families as private individuals. How can this best be handled?

Having drawn up the map the audiences need to be prioritized. Which group is most vital to your interests and which, at least at the moment, can be left alone or the subject of only minor effort? Some of these questions can be best be answered by the next stage.

SLEPT analysis

SLEPT is a simple acronym. It stands for Social, Legal, Environmental, Political and Technological – all issues likely to impact on your organization. Many of the areas overlap but it is worth looking at each separately so as to ensure that all bases are covered.

a) *SOCIAL*: What are the social trends that you need to be aware of? In much of Asia the move from the country to the town is a major issue. This affects not only employment patterns but also traditional family structures, transportation and even voting patterns. A good plan looks to the future rather than bases its actions on data drawn from the past, so it is important that future trends are examined.

b) *LEGAL*: Are you threatened by legislation or is there legislation that you would like to see changed? Should you be considering self-regulation to avoid more formal and potentially heavy-handed legislation from central government? Is the regulatory environment likely to change? In the United States and the United Kingdom, for example, businesses in many sectors such as food, pharmaceuticals, finance and leisure are subject to regulatory bodies that stand one removed from government and cannot therefore necessarily be influenced using conventional political channels. Increasingly, international bodies such as the World Trade Organization (WTO) have an impact here. What are the legal issues that might affect you?

c) *ENVIRONMENTAL*: The environment is likely to be one of the biggest social, political and economic issues of the twenty-first century. How green are you? Do you need to do more and if so how much and how fast? Do you have a crisis plan for environmental disasters? What is your strategy if you are attacked by environmental groups? Environmental issues can be seen very differently in other countries: if such countries feature on your stakeholder map you need to think about *their* environmental concerns.

d) *POLITICAL*: What are the issues that are exciting the politicians? Are you likely to be in the firing line? Do your labor relations match political expectations? Is the government protectionist or laissez-faire? Is the political leadership likely to change and if so in what way? Do you have friends amongst future as well as current leaders? Is power being devolved from the center or taken in?

e) *TECHNOLOGICAL:* Are there developments that are likely to change the way you do business or the way people do business with you? How will you deal with blogs that criticize you? Will you be able to employ sufficient people with the right technological skills to run a sophisticated online service?

By analyzing each of these factors and overlaying it on your stakeholder map you will build up a very thorough view of the organization you represent. This alone will help secure you the ear of senior people and will in turn help you have more influence on the direction of your organization.

All too often PR people are left to communicate the ill-conceived plans of their bosses. Plans that they could have shaped and influenced had they been asked and had the ear of the senior players. A thorough situation analysis helps PR secure a place at the top table.

But even if you are not at the top table and do not have the resources or time to do a full situation analysis, any PR task you are asked or choose to undertake needs a clear set of objectives and that is the stage we move on to next.

CHAPTER 11

Objectives

As we saw in Tables 10.1 and 10.2. PR objectives are subsidiary to the overall organizational objectives. However, like the overall objectives PR objectives, need to be measurable. If they are not measurable how will you know if your PR campaign has worked? (See Evaluation Part II, Chapter 17)

PR objectives can be about behavior and action and about sales and attitudes. Some typical PR objectives are:

- To increase sales of Shiney Shampoo by 10 percent in the next 12 months
- To increase awareness by 15 percent of the need to test themselves for unusual lumps in their breasts or armpits amongst single women under 40
- To get politicians to drop the current proposed legislation affecting your organization
- To increase membership of your organization by 25 percent over the next two years
- To increase donations to your charity by $2,000,000 by 2010
- To increase by 5 percent over the next 12 months the number of children under 5 given a particular vaccination
- To get government to eliminate the illegal trade in specified counterfeit products
- To increase by 50 percent over the next 12 months the volume of positive media coverage about the Chief Executive

SMART objectives

Of course the list is potentially as endless as the types of organizations there are. What unites them all is that they are to a greater or lesser extent **SMART**[1]:

S ... Specific
M ...Measurable
A ... Achievable
R ... Realistic
T ... Timed

Specific

Vague objectives such as, "to launch the new Zoom car successfully" are totally meaningless. How will you know if you have succeeded? Will it be when media coverage of the Zoom car has been achieved or when the Zoom car is the best selling and most profitable car ever? Similarly objectives such as "to raise awareness of the need for a particular vaccination" are little better. How much awareness, and amongst whom? And why awareness? Awareness is no good if people take no action as a result of it. Objectives are no good if they are not specific and measurable.

Measurable

Whether you are talking about media coverage, sales, awareness, or the actions of politicians your objectives should be measurable. However, there are major problems with measurability. These problems can seem so great that PR people are deterred from specifying measurable objectives which in turn leads to accusations that PR is not a proper management discipline like sales or finance. The issue of evaluating PR has preoccupied many people and deserves separate attention: we have explored it in more depth in Part II Chapter 17.

Achievable/Realistic

PR can be a fantastically powerful tool but is badly served by false claims, so make sure that what you are intending is achievable, particularly if you are not in control of all the levers that may affect the outcome, such as price and distribution. If you are being pushed to specify objectives that you feel are unrealistic, try breaking them down into long-term and short-term objectives. So, for example, you might say the long-term objective is to make the Zoom the best-selling car in the market, but your short-term objectives are to get all key motoring journalists to write a review with a view to achieving 30,000 test drives in the first 6 months and 10,000 sales in the first 12 months.

Timed

Timing is an obvious but often neglected aspect of objective setting. A good campaign is reviewed as it goes along so that the lessons can be learnt and changes made, but it is also necessary to have a firm date when a full evaluation of the results can be made. Again the message is to be realistic. Too tight a time frame and your campaign is unlikely to have had a chance to work its full effect, too long a time frame and your campaign is likely to lose direction and energy, if not be forgotten about altogether.

In summary objectives should:
- Describe where you want to get to **not** how you are going to get there (that is strategy).
- Be as SMART as possible. As a minimum they should say WHAT is going to be achieved (measurable) and by WHEN (timed)
- Support the overall organizational objectives (if they do not why are you doing it?)
- Be used to check that all tactics are on strategy and are not simply being undertaken because they will get coverage. It is not being famous that is important but what you are famous for.
- Be clearly linked to the RESULTS section

Objectives are like a thread of steel that runs through any PR proposal from beginning to end.

CHAPTER 12

Strategy

Having chosen the objectives we know where we are going; we now need to know how we are going to get there.

There are some key questions that you need to ask yourself before you devise your strategy. How many of these questions and in how much detail will depend in part on the complexity of the task and in part on how thorough and effective your situation analysis was. The better your situation analysis the easier it will be to devise the strategy.

The questions are:
- **Who is my target *audience*?**
- **What *media* is best for reaching them?**
- **What *message* do I want them to hear and respond to?**
- **What *methods* are best for reaching the target media?**

Audience

Try to be as specific about your audience as possible. For example, simply saying "all shoppers" or "all housewives" is usually too vague. Are they well off or poor? Are they rural or urban? Are they young or old? By answering these questions you can be more precise with your messaging and media selection. You would not, for example, expect to target your mother in the same way as you would target an eighteen-year-old student.

Be wary of saying you want to target everyone or all adults. This is seldom the case and, even when it is the case, there are normally some groups that are more important to you in terms of their influence on others, their spending power or propensity to be receptive to your message. So ask yourself, given a limited amount of money and time, who are the people you *most* want to reach?

There are a number of ways in which an audience can be broken down and profiled for analysis:

Audience profiling

- Age: Try to break down the ages into life stages that affect behavior. For example, teenagers living at home, students away from home, young singles, young couples, young marrieds, young families, families with teenage children, empty nesters – that is adults whose children have left home – early retirees, older retirees and so forth.
- Marital status (e.g. singles, marrieds, divorced)
- Income
- Sex
- Social Class
- Education
- Occupation
- Hobby or interest (e.g. fishing, travel, collecting)
- Social values (e.g. liberal and modern or conservative and traditional)
- Political beliefs
- Religious beliefs
- Geographic location
- Nationality/ethnicity

More often than not, you will need several descriptors to define your target audience. As an example, you may be trying to promote a new sweet tasting premium priced alcoholic drink. The fact that it is premium priced will restrict its appeal to people with high disposable incomes. The fact that is sweet is likely to make it attractive to the young and in particular young women. The fact that it is alcoholic means that it will not appeal to the very religious and socially conservative. Your audience is therefore likely to be aged 18–30; with high disposable income; predominantly but not exclusively, female; socially liberal, and living in a major town or city.

If you are launching a new product or trying to promote a new idea or concept you will need to think about who the key opinion formers are. For example, who are the people who always buy the latest gadgets? Who are the people who influence the uptake of new ideas and influence social behavior?

According to various marketing theorists the consumers or users in most markets can be broken down into distinct groups. These can be described as:

Innovators–Early adopters–Followers–Resisters

If you are entering a new market then clearly the "innovators" and "early adopters" will be key. If, however, you are entering a mature market the biggest potential may lie with the followers. The audience profile of each group is likely to be very different.

As with clearly defining your objectives, clearly defining your audience leads to better results, more efficient use of resources and more accurate evaluation.

Analyzing and defining the audience is usually not too difficult for those working in Marketing PR as the sales and marketing departments often have extensive customer data. If this sort of data is not available you will need to do some market research amongst your target audience, using some or all of the categories above, to find out what they are like and from that determine the best media to reach them through (see later in this chapter).

Targeting a financial or political audience can be more problematic than targeting a consumer audience. For example, let us say you want to change a piece of government legislation currently under consideration. Who do you need to talk to? Is it all politicians or just the ones who have shown an interest in the issue or are against the issue? Who is drafting the legislation? Should you be talking to civil servants and other interested third parties? Is there a local audience that needs to be addressed?

This sort of information is generally much harder to collate and often involves extensive desk research using directories, the Internet, personal contacts, journals, minutes and records. But despite the difficulties, the information can usually be found. Politicians and leaders of charities and NGOs are generally not shy in expressing their views and love to see them in print or on air which means the media itself can be a great market research tool.

One way of categorizing what we can call political audiences is as shown in Table 12.1.

Opposition is those who oppose what you are trying to achieve. You may seek to win them over, ignore or even undermine them.

Table 12.1

Categorizing political audiences		
Opposition	Allies	Neutrals

Allies are those who support, or are likely to support, your goals. Usually it is advisable to work closely with them as the more groups and people you have on your side the more credible and stronger your case will seem to the neutrals.

Neutrals are generally the most important group. It is hard to convert your "enemies" but much easier to win over neutrals. As any politician will tell you the most important voter is a floating voter – the one yet to make up their mind. These are the people who decide elections.

So in summary, you need to research, analyze and then categorize your audiences before you can select the most appropriate media to target them through.

Media

Once the target audience has been defined and analyzed you can start drawing up a media plan. Twenty years ago this was a comparatively easy task. Few countries had more than a couple of TV stations and a dozen or so radio stations. Today most developed nations have literally hundreds of television stations and thousands of radio stations, with magazines and newspapers appealing to every taste and interest. Then of course there is the Internet. In addition to millions of websites there are now blogs and social networks to contend with. At the time of writing there are estimated to be over 30 million blogs worldwide, plus millions of pages on social networks like MySpace and YouTube. Media targeting has got more complicated.

There are two ways of categorizing media – by type or by content.

In most countries media can be broken down into three familiar types. The broadest definition of these types is:

- Broadcast (television and radio, international, national and local))
- Print (newspapers and magazines, international, national and local)
- On-line (websites and blogs)

Beyond the media there is face-to-face communication (parties, seminars, conferences, exhibitions).

However, categorizing by media type is only of limited value as audiences do not just "watch television," they watch particular television programs and read particular newspaper articles and magazines. The nature of media consumption is something that PR practitioners have to think about. It varies in different countries, and even within the same society it evolves over time. In developed countries, for example, newspapers have changed from being relatively expensive products which were shared by many people into relatively cheap and easily discardable. More recently increased television ownership, with multiple sets in individual households, has meant that viewing is less of a group experience, which typically brought together the family. And now television faces the rival attraction of the Internet – very much an individual experience and one that is in many ways at odds with traditional ideas of the mass media: while some websites enjoy heavy traffic, many more are seldom visited and remain much more like books on a library shelf – largely unused but available to those who want them.

People's media preferences are in large part determined by content – and media content generation is at the heart of PR. With more and more media outlets and more and more media available 24 hours a day seven days a week the media is desperate for content. This hunger for content is further fuelled by the economics of modern media which dictates that the minimum number of journalists is employed. In America there are now estimated to be more PR people than there are journalists, and although the PR industries across Asia are much younger it seems clear that numbers of PR people are growing much faster than numbers of journalists. Without PR-created content there would be much less media. Indeed, estimates of the proportion of PR generated news in the United States go as high as 80 percent. In some cases this will be less but in many cases such as fashion and celebrity magazines it is higher.

The Times of India includes pages and supplements for international and Indian business, education, lifestyle, entertainment, health and science, IT, sports, autos, real estate and travel (to name but some). All are looking for content and will welcome good ideas and good stories from PR people.

This proliferation and fragmentation of media offers PR practitioners a fantastic opportunity to get their messages across. After all media organizations want to fill their pages or airtime with the best possible material at the lowest cost, and PR can supply such material at no cost to the media. But in order to take advantage of this opportunity they need to understand the media they are targeting.

In the next chapter on "methods" and in Part III we will look at how to devise media friendly content, but first of all we need to examine the media in a bit more detail.

The first stage is to examine the audience or readership profile of different media to see how well they match your target audience profile. With sophisticated media that are funded in part by advertising this is easily done as the advertising departments of the stations and print titles will have detailed audience profiles which they use to attract advertisers. In many countries this information will also be available from independently produced on-line or print directories produced specifically to help Public Relations practitioners, advertisers and marketers. Alternatively, a direct approach to the targeted title will secure you the information. What is certain is that the broader your target audience is the greater the range of potential media. This is both a problem and an opportunity. An opportunity because it means that there is lots of potential for coverage of your messages, but a problem because prioritizing your media targeting may be a much more time consuming process – unless of course your message is so exciting or your funds so endless that you can afford to target all potential titles equally. This is not a situation that often occurs.

Having profiled the media that best fit your target audience you now need to look at the media's content to see what titles and programs are most likely to cover your story and reach the target audience. Really big stories will be carried on general news pages and programs and carry enormous influence, as news tends to attract vast audiences and have great impact. However, only a minuscule percentage of PR stories will ever make it on to general news so the effective PR practitioner needs to look for richer pastures.

Some media can be described as *vertical*. Media of this sort is dedicated to a particular interest such as sport, fashion or business. Other media can be described as *horizontal* meaning that it covers a wide range of interests from general news to sport, personal finance and home decoration. Newspapers are usually horizontal whilst most magazines are vertical. Television now offers both horizontal content in terms of general channels and vertical in terms of special interest channels like sport and music. On-line media has tended to mimic the television model with a mixture of horizontal and vertical websites. You need to identify and get to know the opportunities in each of your target media be they horizontal or vertical.

Finally, there is what is called "face to face". This covers events owned by others or created by yourself at which the target audience can be reached. These are not really media in the conventional sense of the word, but is nonetheless a vital channel – sometimes the only channel – of communication for your messages.

Like conventional media face-to-face "media" are created to inform, entertain or educate an audience. The numbers of people who can be reached at such events are far less than can be reached by conventional media but are often very powerful because they reach the key opinion formers, innovators and early adopters of new products and ideas.

In the process of drawing up your target audience profile it is quite likely that certain events or exhibitions or shows will have come to your attention. You now need to examine them in the same way that you have examined the other forms of media. For example, in the music arena there are normally a limited number of venues or clubs that are setting the trends. How can you get face to face at these with young opinion formers? At the other extreme most societies have a formal establishment – for example, the government and royal family – and a less formal but nonetheless powerful informal establishment consisting of business people, influential thinkers and writers, academics and certain politicians. Where do these people meet? Is there a dining club, conference or party circuit that you can access?

If there are no appropriate events that you can successfully access can you create one? People of similar interests, be it pop music or power, like to meet each other. Can you help facilitate that meeting and in so doing get your message across?

If all of this conventional media and face to face media analysis sounds very daunting try sitting down with some friends and colleagues and imagine what media your target audience consumes and why and then fill in the Table 12.2 below ... you will probably need at least a page per media type. Once you have filled Table 12.2 use publicly available data to check that your assumptions are correct. In the process you may also find some media you had not thought of.

Table 12.2

Categorizing political audiences		
Type of Media	Name/Title of Medium	Section, Program, Feature, Page
Newspaper • International • National • Local		
Magazine • Consumer • Business • Specialist • Trade (industry specific)		
Television • International • National • Local		
Radio • International • National • Local		
Online • Website • Blog • Social Network		
Face to Face • Exhibitions • Seminars • Conferences • Parties		

In summary, you need to draw up a target media list and then cross-reference that with the particular sections, programs or writers that you want to communicate through. It is also worth bearing in mind that, exceptionally, PR people sometimes have to step beyond the conventional mass media and help people who are producing books or films – something which may be particularly relevant for promoting countries.

Message

A message is basically a communication sent by one organization or person to another. In PR terms it is what you want the audience to read, see or hear as a result of your activity. The successful receipt of a message will ensure that the audience then thinks, feels or does whatever it is that you intended by your activity.

A clear definition of your messages is important for three main reasons:
1. It will give focus to your PR activity ... if it is not "on message" do not do it
2. It will ensure that you have a checklist to use in all communication – including those executed by salespeople or telephone operators
3. It will help make your evaluation more precise

Determining what messages you want to communicate should naturally fall out of your objectives and target audience selection. The clearer your objectives and audience selection the easier it will be to define your messages. But do not just think you can define your message and the rest will take care of itself.

Imagine that you see an attractive member of the opposite sex at a social event and decide that you would like to speak to them. First you must speak in a language they understand. Second, if you are too forward you may repel them, too timid and they may not understand your interest. Their response will also be determined by how they perceive you. What is your reputation? How do you look and dress? Is your tone of voice appropriate to the occasion? And finally their response will be determined by their own values and social confidence. As with all social communication there is much that can go wrong and plenty of room for mistakes and misunderstandings.

Now imagine that it is not you doing the talking but a third party on your behalf! That is what generally happens with Public Relations. You, the sender of the message, relay it to the media who in turn relay it on to the intended recipients (see Figure 12.1) along with a range of other messages that may be more or less interesting to the recipient. Other messages are often called "noise", because, to extend the social event analogy, a lot of background noise can make the message hard or even impossible to hear.

Choosing your messages

So in devising your messages there are at least four things you need to think about:

- *How your organization is perceived.* The language you use and the messages you convey must be interesting and relevant to the audience, but they must also be in keeping with the image and reputation of your own organization. A conservative bank trying to use the language of the street will never sound right. Similarly an organization recently exposed for pollution will not be listened to if they suddenly try to proclaim how green they are.

- *The language and style of the media to be used.* Technical and management language is fine for media that write in that way. In fact very few media titles are technical. Most media, for obvious economic reasons, try to appeal to the broadest possible audience. Use their language and their style. Can the message be expressed in an image or diagram? Not all messages have to be in words.

- *The values, views and language of the recipient.* Generally, media are very sensitive to the values, views and language of their readers, viewers and listeners, so if you have got the previous stage right you are well on the way to getting this stage right. The key thing is to think what will appeal to them? How would they want to hear about this?

- *What are the other messages being communicated at the same time?* The surrounding communications noise can make a big difference to how your message is heard. This can work in two ways. First, there is *competing communication*. Is there a lot going on that might drown out your message? For example, at election time or in times of national crisis the media are often full of hard news that could squeeze out or diminish your news. Similarly, you need to be aware of *contradictory communication*. The key messages you use to communicate a new savings scheme will be very different from what you might have planned following the collapse of a major financial institution that has robbed thousands of their savings.

This information should be readily to hand if you have conducted an effective situation analysis, profiled and defined your target audience and drawn up your target media list.

Think of an organization which you know well. On the basis of its current PR work, try to complete the following Table 12.3. While you may lack all the information that their PR people have, it is nonetheless helpful to start thinking in these terms.

So having considered these factors you now need to write down your messages.

How to express your message

There are two ways of expressing your messages. The first is to express them in the words that you would like the media to use. This is the best route if your evaluation is primarily based on media coverage. *Be realistic* about what the media might say. Most media are not going to publish or broadcast everything you say without

Table 12.3

Planning your messages	
How the organization is perceived	
The language and style of the media to be used	
The values, views and language of the recipients	
What are the other messages which are being communicated at the same time	

criticism. Nor will they, generally, publish it word for word. Indeed, as a general rule the better and more credible the media – and therefore the more effective when they do carry your message – the less likely they are slavishly to do your bidding. Remember that journalists like to see themselves as independent, as people who choose their own angles on stories and their own words, and trampling on this can be counterproductive. You also need to *avoid jargon*, unless targeting a technical audience.

So "Whizzo has a new sub-molecular structure that erases enzymes" should become "Whizzo cleans more, faster." Similarly, "The symbiosis between Whizzcar's technical and sales strategy is predicted to enhance forward growth" becomes "The new Whizzcar is a winner and should sell well." At best, technical and management jargon is useful shorthand for those in the know, at worst it is a barrier to understanding and a smokescreen for sloppy thinking and uninteresting news and ideas. One of your main tasks as a PR person is to try and make your organization understandable to the outside world. The people working there will be very familiar with it, and use jargon accordingly. Not only can this be boring or incomprehensible, but also in some situations it could sound insensitive: imagine an organization talking about a situation which has led to deaths or injuries. You have – diplomatically – to decode and rephrase the words of very senior managers before they reach the media and the public.

The other way of framing your messages is in the language the target audience would use. This is most appropriate when your evaluation includes some tracking studies and benchmark research to see how and if the target audience's attitudes have changed. Sometimes this may correlate directly to the language used by the media but more commonly should be expressed as a "take-out." A take-out is what the recipient of a message says to themselves having received the message. So using our two examples above they might say "Whizzo sounds better than what I am using, perhaps I should give it a try" or "Next time I change the car I will give the Whizzcar a test drive."

In reality the messages you are likely to need to communicate will be more numerous and more complicated than those used above. However, it is important to *have no more than three or four messages* (preferably with one clear over-arching primary message) and *keep all messages clear and simple.*

So, for example, we might say:

Primary Message: Whizzo cleans more, faster.

Secondary messages: Whizzo is based on the latest safe science; Whizzo is made by a firm you can trust; Whizzo is kind to the environment.

Another example might be:

Primary Message: The proposed tram system will move more people more quickly.

Secondary Messages: The tram system will cost no more than the building of the proposed ringroad; the Tram system will reduce pollution by 35 percent in two years; and the opposition to the tram system is financed by the main motor manufacturers.

Clearly for some audiences and some activities the secondary messages will become primary, but in both cases the over-arching key message is clear and simple. The messages are also simple and easy to remember. Bad PR proposals and plans tend to have lots of messages which are impossible to remember, are not relevant or interesting to the audience and sometimes even contradict other messages being communicated elsewhere by the organization.

For an organization that you know well, try to imagine a PR campaign and think of a primary message and secondary message.

Figure 12.1

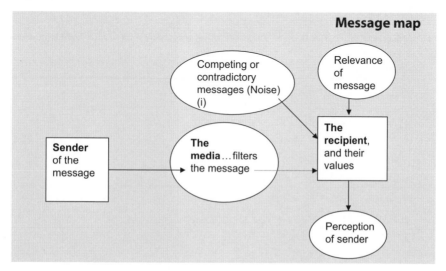

Summary

Think about: (a) how your organization is perceived; (b) the language and style of the media to be used; (c) the values, views and language of the recipient; and (d) what other messages are being communicated at the same time. Also try to: (e) be realistic; (f) avoid jargon; (g) have no more than three or four messages; and keep all messages clear and simple. This is summed up in the Message map, Figure 12.1.

CHAPTER 13

Methods

So we know who our audience is. We have selected our target media and defined our messages. Now we need to think of what methods we are going to use to secure relevant coverage or content in the target media.

There is an enormous number of ways that Public Relations (PR) can be delivered. One of the authors many years ago wrote out a list of possible PR tactics – he gave up when he reached a hundred! Some of these tactics will be outlined in the next section, but what we want to focus on in this part is the categorization of types of activity. We call this the "methods."

Broadly all PR tactics can be categorized into five different types or methods to carry our chosen messages. These are:

- Hard news
- Created or "soft" news
- News events
- Promotional content
- Direct news

Each of these methods is in essence a form of media content. The choice of method or methods will depend on your already completed message and media selection.

Before looking at each of these methods it is worth recalling what the media is looking for.

The media has three simple goals (in addition to making money). That is to *inform, entertain* and *educate*. It is what people read, watch or listen to the media for. The problem is that much of what an organization wants to communicate is not essentially interesting or entertaining and even when it is, their's are not the only messages that the media and ultimately the target audience are being asked to consider. The PR person's job therefore is to take what is often dull or undifferentiated and make it interesting and/or entertaining.

To do this we need to do something called the *180-degree turn*. This involves thinking about what will interest the media and the target audience, rather than what interests the organization, and creating content that will grab their interest whilst successfully carrying the agreed messages. For example computers are not very interesting to many people, but the chance of working from home is. Saving money is not a very interesting subject but luxury goods, holidays and a safe and secure old age are. This is the 180-degree turn, from talking about *me* to talking about *you*, from talking about the organization to talking about the target audience. We can map this out on the Figure 13.1 below.

The best place to be is in the top left hand quadrant. An important and interesting story should be almost guaranteed coverage. The reality is that virtually no story or news is guaranteed coverage, particularly if it has been sent to the wrong media.

Clearly the worst place to be is the bottom right hand quadrant – a place that sadly quite a few organizations find themselves in. However, probably the most common place that organizations find themselves in is the bottom left hand quadrant – important but not interesting. The task of the PR is to make things interesting.

Figure 13.1

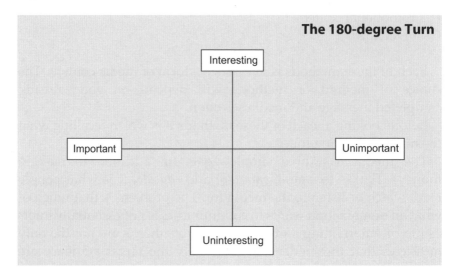

Finally, a word on the top right quadrant. What can be interesting but not important? Well think celebrities, think gossip, think fun and trivia. All these are excellent ways of getting essentially unimportant messages in to the media.

Once again, think back to the organization you know best and think of the kind of announcements it makes. Where would they fit into this figure?

Hard news

"Hard news" is a newspaper term. It means news that relates to real events of real importance. The outbreak of wars, the calling of elections, and the discovery of murders are all front page news for national newspapers and TV news programs. Very occasionally a company will make the front pages with a "good news" story, perhaps for a new invention, a dramatic rise in profits or the hiring of a lot of staff. More commonly they will make the front page because of financial or product failures – and often this amounts to a crisis which threatens the very existence of the company (see Crisis Management, Part II Chapter 18).

Of course what is considered hard news is different when it comes to specialist media or specialist sections in general titles. For example a healthy growth in profits for a national computer company is likely to be covered by the business pages of the national print media, the computer trade magazines, the specialist business and financial media – including online media – and local press around the company's main offices and factories. But it is very unlikely to get any coverage on a news bulletin on a popular music channel.

Even if you have a news story or stories you need to present it in a way that ensures that busy news desks spot it. "Computer Firm publishes financial results," is unlikely to grab the attention of a harassed journalist. On the other hand, "Profits double for computer giant" might just do the trick provided it has been sent at the right time and to the right people. Similarly, a new product may be of interest in its own right but is even more likely to get coverage if it is supported with a great photograph, particularly if it is one of a celebrity.

When drawing up your plan you need to make a realistic appraisal of how much "hard news" you are likely to have over the time period of your plan. It is always worth remembering that what is considered no news at all by one medium may be considered very hard news by another, for example, a specialist media outlet. The key is to be realistic in your assessment of what news is and who is likely to find it so.

Hard news which an organization is likely to want to promote includes:

- New products
- New services
- Expansion (more people, shops or factories)
- A new boss
- New discovery or new research that changes the way people think

And then of course there are plenty of more negative hard news stories, but to deal with them see Part III, Chapter 20.

Try to think of likely positive hard news stories for the organization you know best. What stories would *have* to be covered by which media?

If the answer to your audit of hard news possibilities is "not a lot" you will need to consider some or all of the methods outlined below.

As Asian brands export more they will become more involved in arranging press trips for journalists from other countries ...

While press trips can be fun, the poorly arranged ones do stick in people's minds. One editor of a gadget magazine was recently taken on a seven-day tour of Asia. The pace of the trip – with briefings as soon as the editor landed – was described as "tortuous" with no relaxation time.

To avoid this and get the best return on investment the media relations manager of another company says they conduct rigorous evaluation of every trip to ensure it achieves objectives.

"We look at short, mid and long-term coverage, and at whether the right messages have been communicated. If they haven't, we re-evaluate our invite list and approach."

Bite, a PR consultancy, says: "We regularly arrange press trips for Samsung to Korea, as there is interest in seeing how they design and develop their products at their R&D centres in Seoul. The trips are tailored to individual journalists and detailed itineraries are worked out to make sure the trip is worthwhile, gives an angle relevant to their publication and justifies a long journey."

Source: PR Week

Created or "soft" news

Created or "soft" news is also sometimes called "news out of nothing." Typical examples of created news are:

- Surveys, research, and interesting facts and figures
- Predictions of future trends
- Psychological profiles of different types of people relevant to your market
- Guide books designed to help people with relevant problems or activities

PR companies themselves can use survey data to garner useful publicity. This story appeared in *The Times of India*:

Global business executives assign nearly 60 percent of the blame to CEOs when companies lose reputation after a crisis strikes, while it is slightly less – 55 per cent-for India.

The finding did not significantly differ among the other regions, according to a Safeguarding Reputation survey carried out by attitudinal research firm KRC Research and global Public Relations firm, Weber Shandwick.

Regardless of region, executives consider financial wrongdoing and unethical behavior the most significant threats to reputation. Compared to their counterparts in other regions, however, Asian executives are more sensitive to factory breakdowns or explosions, North Americans to environmental issues, and Europeans to health and safety product recalls.

Created news is a very popular method when an organization is likely to have little hard news. Commonly this will apply to well-established companies or marketplaces when there is little new to say. Let us take the example of a mobile phone company.

In markets where there is genuine competition between companies the media and the consumer are subjected to a constant barrage of new services and offers. Most are instantly copied and many rarely get a media mention other than in paid for advertising. So how does the clever company keep its name at the forefront of the media and consumers mind? The answer is often research. Sometimes this will be data that the company has gathered naturally in the course of its business, sometimes it will be data that it has collected specially – often through a specialist research firm – that tells us something new about the market and its consumers. This sort of activity can be called anything from a report, survey, and index through to a study or even a strategic discussion paper. At its heart is research and data. The media love facts and figures.

For example, the mobile phone company may have data that shows what kind of people buy which kinds of phones. It might even employ a psychologist to say what your choice of phone says about you as a person. Alternatively it may commission research to find out what the most common kinds of text messages are and whether people have used text to arrange a date or finish a relationship.

And it is not just consumer product firms that can use research to create news. Insurance companies can tell us what sorts of businesses are most likely to suffer fire or crime. NGOs can use research to show what people's attitudes are to particular social problems and accountancy firms can use research to talk about business trends. Often organizations are sitting on a gold mine of information if only they thought of using it. In the UK insurance companies – hardly the most interesting product area – have revealed everything from how star signs seem to influence the likelihood of having an accident or choice of car color through to the most bizarre excuses for having had an accident and the most popular music played at funerals.

Another way of creating news is to make predictions of future trends: the media adores speculation about what lies ahead. So food retailers can talk about future eating trends, medical companies can talk about twenty-first century diseases and NGOs can predict the effects of global warming, declines in animal populations or increases in specific kinds of poverty.

As touched on above, psychology is another way of creating news out of nothing. Is your future mother-in-law a lion, a snake, a cat or mongoose? When the question is presented by a bridal ware company who could resist finding out? Or from a firm of business advisers, "are you a leader, innovator, manager or outcast?" None of this is really hard news but it is interesting – we all have egos – even if it is seldom actually important.

Then there are guidebooks. As with the use of psychologists these are often supported by some research data. For example, our mobile telephone company could produce a guide on "Long Distant Love ... how to keep in touch when your loved one is far away." A funeral company could produce a guide on how to handle bereavement and a car company could produce a guide to the ten best scenic drives in the country.

All these are examples of news created by PR people for the purpose of securing media coverage to convey key messages. All are also examples of things that are informative, entertaining and educational. Just what the media asked for.

The Advertising Studies School at the Communication University of China conducted a survey of 235 PR people and asked how they thought the Beijing Olympics would affect public relations in China. Not surprisingly the view was very positive. More interestingly this was a very good piece of PR for the Communication University of China and effectively created news where there had been none.

Source: China.org.cn

News events

These are events that are created to make otherwise rather weak news stories stronger or are created to generate news in their own right. For example, a cosmetic company is launching a new perfume. There is not much in fact that the media can usually say about a new perfume: it is, after all, fantastically difficult to describe a smell. So to grab the media's attention the perfume company holds a party to which top celebrities are invited. The release of a new record by a well established star might be spiced up with an invitation to the media to see them perform in an unusual location like a children's home or a prison. A firm launching a new motorcycle safety suit might simulate a dramatic crash in a densely populated city center. Or a bottle making company might decide to create a large-scale model of a famous building out of glass bottles, thus ensuring plentiful exposure for its name and enhancing its reputation as company with new ideas. Care has always to be exercised as eye-catching ideas can attract the wrong kind of publicity. For example in 2007 the President of Cartoon Network had to resign following a publicity stunt which went seriously wrong and triggered a bomb alert in Boston.

Using celebrities and soap operas

Nobody can underestimate the power of soap operas, especially in Southeast. But they are just as likely to be a force for good as anything else.

Governments, development agencies and civil society groups all use television and film personalities to get their messages across to a mass audience effectively.

The United Nations program for combating Aids – UNAids – announced that mixing HIV prevention messages with serial dramas was a proven model for combating the growth of HIV infection.

"The role of television personalities in South East Asia is far greater than their equivalent in Europe and the US," said a leading Asian PR executive

"Market research shows that ... TV stars endorsements are essential to sell consumer products like cosmetics, drinks and so on."

Source: www.bbc.co.uk

Politicians seem particularly adept at the news event. An announcement on a small increase in funding for school sports that might otherwise have gone unnoticed is suddenly a news event when the minister launches it by playing five minutes of football with a school team. (Once again this sort of approach is apt to back fire if the minister overrates his own footballing prowess and falls flat on his face).

By knowing your media you will quickly get to know what sort of events get coverage and in Part III, Chapter 27 we describe in a bit more detail how to create an effective PR photograph or photo opportunity.

Promotional content

Promotional content includes activities such as:

- competitions
- giveaways
- sponsored pages, supplements and programs.

Promotional content is different from standard media relations in that it involves the provision of goods or money to the host media. Some even argue that such activities are not proper PR and should be under the control of advertising agencies. The authors believe these sorts of turf wars are unhelpful. The owner of the activity should surely be the person best able and qualified to execute it. Promotions are different from advertising in that they are usually conducted in the editorial style of the host media. PR people if properly trained should be expert in the editorial style of the host media and also have useful contacts with the relevant journalists.

Promotional content is unlikely to be used as the sole method of PR communication, but is an increasingly popular approach because, first, the media in its thirst for content welcomes it and, second, because it guarantees the inclusion of your messages, usually in a way that you can control. So, for example, a driving school in conjunction with a media title with good reach amongst young people who are old enough to start learning to drive may run a competition in which readers or viewers have to recognize the profile of famous cars. The winners get free driving lessons and the driving school gets branded coverage and very positive mentions of their successful pass rates. If the competition is run over a number of weeks the medium gets not only reader interest but also loyalty, as the readers have to buy each issue.

Similarly a health company may sponsor – and help write – a column of health tips in a woman's magazine and our perfume company may offer 100 free bottles of perfume to the first 100 readers to write in.

A tourist authority may sponsor a whole travel supplement featuring holidays in its particular country, or a national business organization or government may sponsor a supplement containing articles about its country as a business destination and place to invest.

The benefits in all these cases are the implied endorsement and approval of your product by the media partner, positive descriptions of whatever it is you are "selling" (if it is good enough to be a prize it must be good!) and in certain cases the collection of names and addresses for future contact.

Direct news

Direct news is about taking or sending your messages directly to your target audience. This can be as simple as sending a report or paper outlining your position on an issue to a select group of influential politicians, through to holding a massive celebrity-filled party or organizing a major conference. This may sound like a repetition of what was described under News events and in some ways it is. The difference is that with Direct news any media coverage is a secondary objective, the primary objective being to reach the target audience directly without the mediating influence of the media.

This sort of activity is, as we observed when looking at face-to-face media, expensive. The cost per audience contact when compared with a conventional media campaign that might reach millions for fractions of a penny per head are very high, but so too are the potential returns. Direct news can be cost effective. A group of celebrities being exposed to your product and turning into ambassadors for it is almost incalculable in value. Similarly, a major conference involving planners and political and business leaders on the future of urban transportation will ensure the organizers – the foremost firm in the development of trams – make contact with the people most able to influence their future success. Resulting media coverage is just a bonus.

Exercise. Try to think of examples of how each of the above techniques could be used for your chosen organization.

Having defined the Methods to be used we can now look at the art of being creative.

CHAPTER 14

How to be creative

This is chapter is divided into three main parts:

1. How to create a creative environment
2. How to run a successful brainstorm
3. How to turn great ideas into effective PR activity

How to create a creative environment

Creativity is all about inspiration is it not? You just sit at your desk and creative ideas will come to you. The reality is very different. This may sound like a contradiction in terms but creativity needs to be planned.

There used to be a famous golfer called Arnold Palmer. One day a sports journalist said to him that he thought he was very lucky. Palmer replied, "And the more I practice the luckier I get." Sometimes people describe footballers who score a lot of goals as lucky. But how lucky are they? To score a goal you have to be in the right place at the right time and finish with enough skill to beat the goalkeeper. Great Public Relations (PR) people are the same. They have to combine experience, a positive attitude and skill to achieve success. Creativity in PR is 90 percent perspiration and 10 percent inspiration.

How to have a creative attitude

To be creative you need a creative attitude, but what is a creative attitude? Well there are certain attributes and habits which are essential:

- Be open minded
- Be interested in other people's lifestyles and ideas

- Be familiar with the media
- Realize that your life is untypical of many groups in society

SO

- Consume a wide variety of media (read the papers and magazines, watch TV, go to the cinema, surf the world wide web (WWW), experience the blogosphere and get out and do things)
- Think about how to turn information into media stories
- Watch out for and make a note of new trends and ideas
- Look for things that touch people's hearts *and* minds
- Watch and learn from what the competition is doing
- Challenge conventional thinking

If you work in a team, or have colleagues you think would be interested, have a half hour meeting once a fortnight (first thing on a Monday morning is a good time) and ask them all to bring along an article, news story or video clip that has made them think differently about something.

Try and make your office a creative space. Stick up articles and images that encourage and inspire people to have ideas.

Rules of brainstorming

A brainstorm is like a meeting only much more fun!

The purpose of a brainstorm is to get together a group of people to generate new ideas. At the end of the brainstorm you should have a range of ideas you can develop into full-blown PR tactics. Like any sort of meeting, if a brainstorm is to be effective it needs to be planned in advance. There are some basic rules that need to be followed.

People

A maximum of about seven people is best. Too many people and it becomes hard to control and hard to include a contribution from everyone (and there is nothing worse and more energy sapping than people sitting in silence throughout a brainstorm).

All the attendees should be looking forward to being there. It is hard to be creative if you are in a bad mood. So make sure when you invite people you make it sound fun and that it is a bit of a compliment that they have been invited. And once they are there praise them.

Do not just use people from the PR or marketing team. Bring in people from elsewhere in the organization, or even outsiders if possible. They may bring a fresh perspective, particularly if they are drawn from the target audience you are looking at. You would not expect a 70-year old to be very good at coming up with ideas to target 20-year olds and yet all too often a group of people in their twenties try to come up with ideas to target 70-year olds.

Try not always to use the same people in brainstorms because if you do you will tend to end up getting the same sort of ideas.

Finally, appoint someone to keep notes of all the ideas. You will be too busy encouraging and stimulating ideas to record them as well.

Location/Atmosphere

Offices are not great places for brainstorms. People are easily distracted by phone calls or someone wanting "a quick word." Offices also induce a "work" frame of mind which is very goal orientated. In the office you are asked a question, you give an answer. But brainstorms are not about answers but ideas. So if you can try to have your brainstorm offsite it will make people more relaxed and more prepared to think outside of the box.

Even if you have to have the brainstorm in the office remember it does not have to take place around a table. If there is an area with some comfortable chairs use that. And think about providing some refreshments. It is hard to think when you are thirsty or hungry. Also remember to bring along samples of any product being discussed as well as copies of the media you are targeting. This will all help the participants get in the right mood.

Finally, provide people with a notepad and pen and encourage scribbling and doodling. It all helps people get in the right frame of mind.

Structure

How you structure your brainstorm is critical. The best structure has three phases:

SCOPE————GENERATE————EVALUATE

At the start of the brainstorm, having welcomed everyone, you need to scope the subject being brainstormed. This means describing the background to the topic under discussion and what you want to achieve from the brainstorm. It is important in the scoping stage not to give too much detail, as this tends to confine people's thinking. It is also important for the same reason not to burden participants with previous problems, or your own preconceived ideas about what is needed or what will or will not work.

Once you have scoped the topic you can move on to the ideas generation. At this stage it is vital that no idea is criticized however impractical or daft it may seem. Even seemingly bad ideas can stimulate good ideas. Moreover, as soon as an idea has been criticized the less confident people in the group will tend to clam up, fearing that if they come up with an idea it will be criticized.

When people do come up with an idea thank them and make a note of the idea, even if you think you are never going to use it. This will stimulate others to contribute ideas. In the unlikely event that the ideas really are going off track just gently nudge people back on track without appearing to denigrate the ideas already noted. This seeming acceptance of ideas that are off target goes against most business instincts. In business the emphasis is usually on accuracy – the right answer as soon as possible. But in the generation phase of a brainstorm we are not looking for the right answer. Instead, we are looking for a range of answers so we can choose the best. Psychologists will confirm that the creative part of the brain is different from the critical part. We find it very difficult to be creative and critical at the same time which is why in brainstorming the critical phase is left to last and is kept distinct from the generating phase.

To help you with the generating phase there are a number of different types or styles of brainstorm and these are described later in this chapter.

The third and final phase of a brainstorm is the evaluation phase. Some people prefer to keep this entirely separate from the brainstorm. They simply thank everyone for all their ideas and then take the ideas away and in the privacy of their own office decide which to develop. This might be sensible if most of the participants are not PR or communication people but is unnecessary if most of the participants are communication literate.

A good way of evaluating the ideas is to write them up on large sheets of paper and stick them up around the room. Then ask the participants to put dot stickers or a big tick on the ideas they like the most. Having done that ask the participants to sit down again and discuss with them the ideas that have come out on top and why. By the end of the session you should have a range of workable outline ideas recorded.

How to turn these ideas into effective PR activity is covered in the last section of this chapter.

Cultural differences emerge in meetings

Hill and Knowlton's Human Resources Manager for China commented:

"Generally speaking foreign staff are more extroverted than local ones, but they need to be more patient when working with local staff.

When we have a meeting, I normally ask the staff if they have any questions or problems … then most of the Chinese staff keep silent. But, after the meeting they will come to me to ask questions."

Source: Yujie He, University of Westminster MA thesis

Types of brainstorming

There are a variety of types of brainstorm. We have decided to focus on three that we have found particularly useful.

Future-thinking

This is a simple but highly effective technique. The first stage is to think of at least five trends or issues that could affect your organization's market or consumers in the future. Most research is about the past when what people really want to know about is what will happen in the future. For example, if you were in the motor industry you might predict that: (a) more women are going to learn to drive and have their own cars; (b) that there may be legislation to outlaw polluting or very big engines; (c) that traffic congestion will encourage a return to two wheels; (d) more families will own cars; and (e) that there will be increased demand for pedestrianized shopping areas.

Having made your predictions you now try to generate some PR ideas. For example, you might produce a report on women drivers, how many there are, how many there will be and how they are different from male drivers, perhaps with a comment from a psychologist. Alternatively, you could ask a group of women to design the perfect car and have a model made up of it to show to the press. To show you care about pollution and congestion why not create and sponsor an award for the best pedestrianized shopping center, or link up with a foldaway bike company and devise a special promotion in media read by commuters.

Random association

This technique is particularly good when you have been working for a long time on something and the ideas seem to have dried up.

Just think of two words. Ideally one should be an object and the other a living thing. So, for example, you might choose a suitcase and an orange. You then just ask people to call out any words that come to mind related to your two key words. This might give you a list as shown below in Table 14.1.

At first glance a very random selection of words. But imagine you are a firm of lawyers (solicitors) and look again. Look first at the words under suitcase.

You could do an article on how the law is trying to keep up with money laundering and online smuggling. You could do a survey of how many people's holidays or travel plans are ruined by rogue operators and give hints and tips on how to get your money back. Or looking at "orange" you could compare legal practice in your own country with that in Florida in the USA. You could look at the legality of the football transfer market or offer a mobile phone-based

Table 14.1

Example of random association	
Suitcase	Orange
• Clothes	• Florida
• Travel	• Holland Football Team
• Protection	• Bad sun tan
• Airplanes	• Mobile phones
• Money in the suitcase	• Juice
• Smuggling	• Zest
• Holidays	• Vitamin C

rapid response legal service. Almost every word seems to have the potential to generate ideas for an organization that a few moments before seemed the dullest on earth.

Talking walls

Scope the problem or issue first (remember not to provide too much information) then give them five minutes in silence to come up with one idea and ask them to write it on the top of a large piece of paper. Stick the paper up around the room and then get everyone to walk around and add a comment or new idea to each piece of paper. It is amazing how the original idea stimulates further ideas. This technique is also particularly good for getting normally shy but creative people to contribute.

You can also mix and match techniques. For example, you could use the first part of random association to generate some words then write those words on sheets and stick them up around the room for people to add their ideas to. Similarly, you could take the future trends generated using future thinking and write them on the sheets to be added to.

And here are a few other techniques you can try.

- Bite-sized brainstorms (just two or three people for 15 or 20 minutes)
- Brainstorms on the move (get out of the office and go for a walk with two or three other brainstormers)
- Use TV soap operas as the springboard for ideas. What would they think about your product or service?
- Think up advertising ideas and then turn them into PR ideas

Exercise. Using a chosen organization as a springboard, get together with some colleagues or friends and try brainstorming ideas for an imaginary PR campaign. Try to use as many of the methods described above as you can.

Turning ideas into activity

The first thing to do is have another look at the five main methods described in Part II, Chapter 14.

- Hard news
- Created "soft" news

- News events
- Promotional content
- Direct news

Now think about the core story behind your idea. What is the target audience problem or issue you are addressing? What is the solution or help that you are offering? What is in it for the media?

Does the idea have some of the key elements of a great media story?

- Conflict, controversy, money, health, sex, crime, glamor
- Facts, figures or trends
- Expert views, advice or predictions
- Celebrities
- A great photograph or visual
- Case histories/human interest

Imagine you are doing the PR for a new kind of handbag that can only be opened by scanning the owner's fingerprint. You have had an excellent brainstorm that has focused on the fear of crime and now you are drafting out your ideal story. Would it read something like this?

Women are now more frequent victims of street robbery than men, according to a new report

The report, published by Securebag, makers of secure handbags for women, reveals that one in ten women will have their handbag stolen this year. Mr Green, Securebag's security consultant said: "Street robbery is reaching near epidemic proportions in some areas and looks set to increase by a further 25 percent over the next two years unless people start taking action to protect themselves."

Last week in London Miss Megastar was robbed outside her Chelsea home. Mr Green commented: "Her security guard was no help. The bag snatcher was gone before the guard could react."

Lorna Li of Bangkok (see picture) was robbed last year and now always uses a Securebag. She said: "with street crime on the increase I think it makes sense to do everything you can to deter robbers. Fortunately the bags are very stylish too."

In under 200 words this story has all the key elements – drama, facts, experts, celebrities (and they have not had to be paid) and a human-interest case history. It also conveys a very positive message for Securebags. However, there may be more that can be done with this story.

The final stage is to check if you have covered all the media opportunities. Is it tailored for different audiences? Think about how you can:

- *Sectorize your story*: For example, if you have a computer-based story you can tailor it for every industry sector that uses computers which nowadays is just about every industry, from pharmaceuticals to sewage processing.
- *Regionalize your story*: The more local you can make a story the better. If you are using research, for example, try to break down the figures by province or region and lead your story with the figure that makes that province look the best or worst.
- *Do business and consumer versions*: All consumer-focused stories have a business angle of some sort. Is what you are doing to target consumers of interest to other businesses?
- *Visualize your story*: What could you do to make this a story that would appeal to television?
- *Asset strip your story*: Could you turn this into two or even three separate stories.

The Securebags story could certainly be tailored for regional media, business press and fashion media. Some film of a thief trying to open a Securebag might also win the story some TV coverage.

Exercise. Think up an imaginary story about a new product or service available from your chosen organization. Can you give it all the characteristics of a successful news story?

CHAPTER 15

Tactics

Tactics are the delivery mechanisms of Public Relations (PR). They carry the messages to the target audience. But they succeed only if they are the right tactics for the chosen media and have content that is attention grabbing. Press releases, surveys or photo opportunities are no good in themselves if they do not secure coverage. It is the idea behind them that is all-important.

In the last chapter we looked at how to create memorable and effective ideas. In this chapter we are going to have a look at the variety of tactics available to the PR practitioner to communicate their creative ideas.

The Table 15.1 is designed to indicate some of the tactics that can be used for each of the "methods" discussed in the previous chapter. Inevitably this list cannot be exhaustive. It is also the case that some of the tactics can be used with some or all of the methods.

As you may have noticed some of the above tactics overlap with other disciplines like advertising, direct mail and sales promotion. This is particularly true in the marketing Public Relations (MPR) sector. Occasionally this leads to turf wars within organizations. It should not. It should instead encourage close cooperation between teams and where appropriate cross skills working (see Figure 15.1).

The thing to remember with all of these tactics is that they must be backed by great ideas. Content is king and content is where the creative flair comes in. Indeed creativity is what makes PR so different from other management disciplines. PR people, like lawyers and accountants, research and analyze and have planning systems, but unlike lawyers and accountants PR people also need creative flair. They have to produce ideas that turn the mundane and ordinary in to the exceptional and exciting. It is one of the things that makes PR such a popular and attractive occupation.

Table 15.1

Methods and tactics matrix	
Method (How are we going to get there?)	Tactics (What are we going to do?)
HARD NEWS	Press conference Press briefing Press release Video news release
CREATED "SOFT" NEWS	Survey Psychologists' Report Predictions Index Study Guidebook Charitable donations/sponsorship (These sorts of tactics are actually delivered using a combination of news releases, articles, briefings, interviews and features)
NEWS EVENTS	An unusual event (oldest, newest, biggest, fastest, oddest etc.) Celebrity presence A major party Fashion show (These sorts of events usually have a strong visual element and are popular with TV and picture editors)
PROMOTIONAL CONTENT	Editorial competition Product giveaways Product placement Sponsored pages or columns Advertorial (An advertisement done in editorial style)
DIRECT NEWS	Exhibitions Conferences Seminars Briefings Hospitality/Entertainment Special reports Special newsletter, video, DVD, web link

Figure 15.1

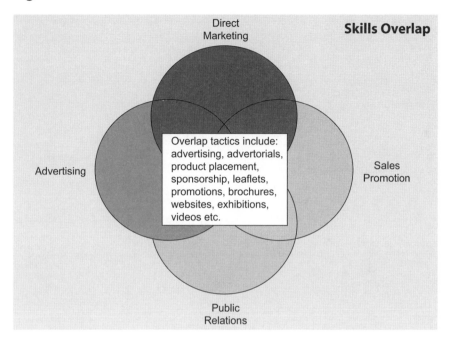

Skills Overlap

Direct Marketing

Advertising

Sales Promotion

Public Relations

Overlap tactics include: advertising, advertorials, product placement, sponsorship, leaflets, promotions, brochures, websites, exhibitions, videos etc.

Table 15.2

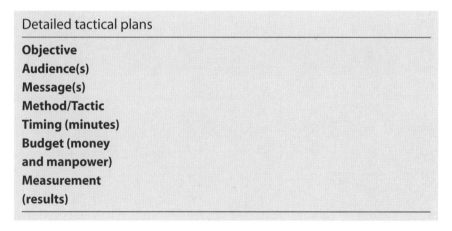

Detailed tactical plans
Objective
Audience(s)
Message(s)
Method/Tactic
Timing (minutes)
Budget (money and manpower)
Measurement (results)

Having decided on your methods and tactics you can start to draw up a detailed tactical plan. The next few sections will help you consider the money, minutes and manpower issues covered under the ACTION section of the POSTAR plan, shown here as "Timing" and "Budgets," as well "as measurement" (Table 15.2).

CHAPTER 16

Administration

In this chapter we look at what we need to achieve our objectives in terms of *Manpower, Minutes and Money*.

In the last chapter we eulogized over the creative element of Public Relations (PR), but creativity is nothing without rigorous systems and, in particular, tight budgeting. Sadly, too many PR practitioners forget this and in so doing undermine their standing with senior and financial managers. Much of this can be overcome by understanding a simple business formula called the *time, cost, quality equation*. This equation is particularly important to PR consultants who are selling their time, but it is also useful to in-house PR people who still need to justify their own salaries and those of their teams and manage their workload and priorities.

The time, cost, quality equation (see Figure 16.1) dictates that the buyer of any service can only determine two of the three factors. So if they want high quality they must accept that either it will be at a premium price or that it will take longer to execute. Similarly, if they want low cost they must accept that either timing or quality will be affected. Service providers who promise to do the best job at the lowest price in the quickest time will end disappointing the buyer and will quite probably end up out of pocket themselves. It cannot be done.

In fact, the first thing a PR person trying to cost a PR program needs to do is decide if they have the right people for the job.

Manpower

There are four broad skill areas that are needed in PR:

- *Strategic skills* (the ability to liaise with senior management, understand and analyze business objectives and translate this into an effective PR strategy)

- *Management/Administrative skills* (the ability to plan, manage, cost and follow up people and activity)
- *Technical skills* (for example, writing, designing and selling stories to journalists)
- *Creative skills* (the ability to come up with new content ideas)

In small organizations you may be called upon to play all roles. In larger organizations there is a greater opportunity to specialize. In reality, most people are only good at two or at most three of these areas. (How many people do you know who are both very creative and very well organized and efficient? These attributes require different parts of the brain and are seldom equally balanced in one individual.) If you, or your team, are lacking in some of these skills you will need to think about where you can get them from. Can someone with the right skills be seconded, or do you need to hire a specialist?

Figure 16.1

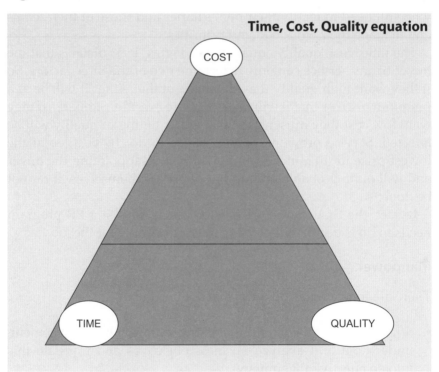

Any buyer of services can only demand to control two of the three factors.

Manpower measurement

Having got the right mix, you now need to assess how much time will be required of each of the team. To do this you need some form of measurement of time. This is best done via timesheets. Without timesheets you can only guess at how much time any particular activity will take. By using timesheets from previous activities you will much more accurately be able to predict, for example, how long it takes to devise, commission and analyze a piece of research, then write it up, get it approved and send it to the media.

Time is often the biggest cost in any PR campaign. If you cannot realistically estimate the time that a project is going to take you cannot realistically cost that project. Time sheets are an essential management tool (Table 16.1).

The choice of headings should be based on the kind of work you do, but it is well worth including a "meetings" heading. Whilst meetings have their role, they can also use up an enormous amount of time. Only when you use time sheets can you be certain just how much time and therefore cost is needed.

Timesheets should be collected each day. It is even better if they are loaded on to people's computers so that they cannot log off until the timesheet is completed. Timesheets should then be analyzed and

Table 16.1

Detailed tactical plans					
	Planning	Writing	Meetings	Administration	TOTAL HOURS
News Event					
Media Promotion					
Research based created news					
TOTAL					

discussed on a monthly basis. Slowly a very clear picture will emerge of how much time, on average, different PR activities take.

Minutes (Time!)

There are three aspects to devising a time plan. The first is to know how long particular tasks are going to take, and this has been covered in the section above on manpower measurement and timesheets. The second aspect of timing is much harder to measure. That is how quickly, or slowly, your organization can approve and action a program. (Generally the bigger the organization the more slowly it moves). The third aspect requires you to consider external time factors. For example, will your activity clash with some big event and therefore be squeezed out of the media? When is the optimum time to undertake your activity? New Year stories just after New Year do not work. Similarly, there is little point doing a story on storm protection just after the monsoons. All these points need to be considered.

Essentially there are three stages to drawing up a time plan.

Stage One: The first stage is to *identify the key tasks*. This involves breaking the program down into its component parts. So, for example, you need to allow time for planning and creating the program. You then need to allow time to present it internally to ensure you get funding and support from those who matter and then, finally, there is the execution phase. How long will it actually take to complete each of the activities?

Stage Two: The second stage is to *draw up a critical path analysis (Figure 16.2)*. This entails understanding which activities are time critical. For example, if you are building a house you cannot do anything until the foundations are in place and there is no point in plastering the walls until the wiring is installed. The same applies to PR. If the research is late, the created news story will be late. If the celebrity is not booked by a certain date you may not be able to secure their services or have time to print a program with their name in.

Figure 16.2 shows a *critical path analysis* for a simple guidebook that has to be ready for 30 April.

Stage Three: The third stage is to check the plan against the calendar for known (or, where possible, likely events) such as elections, major

Figure 16.2

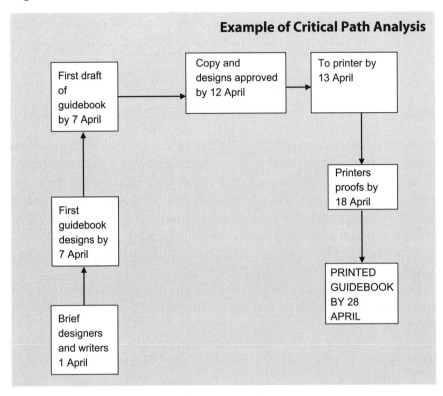

Example of Critical Path Analysis

First draft of guidebook by 7 April → Copy and designs approved by 12 April → To printer by 13 April

First guidebook designs by 7 April → First draft of guidebook by 7 April

Brief designers and writers 1 April → First guidebook designs by 7 April

To printer by 13 April → Printers proofs by 18 April → PRINTED GUIDEBOOK BY 28 APRIL

Table 16.2

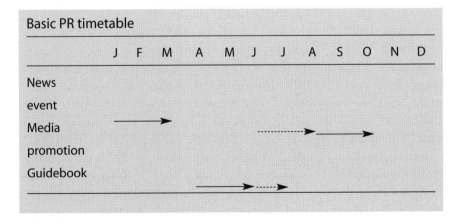

Basic PR timetable

	J	F	M	A	M	J	J	A	S	O	N	D
News												
event												
Media												
promotion												
Guidebook												

sporting competitions, seasonal activity such as public holidays and of course your own organization's and competitors' activity.

You will now be able to draw up a proper calendarized timetable for your whole PR program for the year. Table 16.2 shows a much-simplified version.

All that needs to be dealt with now is the money.

Money

In some cases you will have little say in the overall budget which will have been determined by the chief executive or finance director based on previous practice or as a percentage of sales or a percentage of the overall marketing budget. If this is the case you will have to tailor your program to the money you have. If you are luckier you will be allowed to work out what you think needs to be done, cost it out and present it for approval. In reality, many budgets are determined by some combination of the two.

Whatever situation you find yourself in, the more accurately you can estimate the costs of any program the more successful you are likely to be.

There are three elements to the costs of any PR campaign. They are:
- People costs
- Physical costs (like design, print, celebrity fees and research)
- Expenses (photocopying, phones and postage)

People costs

Whether you work for an in-house PR team or a PR consultancy, people are usually your biggest cost. There are two aspects to people costs. The first is of course salary, and many PR budgets are expressed simply based on this cost, but there is also a range of secondary costs entailed with the employment of anyone. These secondary costs include holidays, training, employment taxes, pensions and the physical space consumed within the office and the cost of accounts, receptionists and other support staff. Broadly you can estimate that, in total, someone costs twice their salary.

However, many consultancies in the West work on the **three-thirds principle**. This principle dictates that a third of costs are salary; a third overheads, including all the factors mentioned above; and a third profits. In reality profits in excess of 30 percent of income are very rare, around 13 percent is much more common, but this does not undermine the value of the three-thirds principle as a goal. It also explains why consultancy costs can at first glance look very high.

Another way of working out the overhead cost per person is to take the total number of employees in your organization and then divide the total overhead costs by that number. This will give you an overhead cost per employee. From this you can work out an average cost per hour per PR employee. You should now be able to estimate the real people cost for any PR program.

Physical Costs

These are all the extra costs generated as a result of the campaign ranging from research and printing through to celebrity fees and the hire of locations for events. PR consultancies will sometimes add a mark-up of between 10 and 15 percent to these costs to cover the cost to them of administering the purchases and financing the cost until they are paid by the client.

It is important to negotiate the best prices for these physical costs whilst remembering the principles of the *time, cost, quality equation* mentioned on page 107. Good work is seldom the cheapest.

A well-organized PR person keeps a record of all supplier quotes so that they can build up a data bank of possible prices to help with the costing of future projects.

Finally, there are expenses.

Expenses

There are three ways to cover for expenses such as phones, photo-copying and postage.

- The first is to record them accurately and charge in arrears accordingly.
- The second is to make an estimate based on past experience and quote that. (However, this can be a risky business as you cannot always precisely control these costs.)
- The third is to base expenses on a percentage of the time cost. So, for example, if the time cost is to be ten per cent of the total time available over the year then ten percent of the expenses incurred over that period should be charged to the project.

An outline PR budget may therefore look like this (Table 16.3):

The plan is now nearly complete. All that remains to complete our POSTAR is to show how we intend to tell whether we have succeeded or not. In other words, how we will measure our results.

Table 16.3

Outline PR budget	
Cost item	Actual cost
People Costs (100 hours at $50.00)	$5,000
Physical Costs	
1. Guidebook (writing, design and print)	$3,000
2. Psychologist's fee	$500.00
3. Research	$500.00
Expenses	$ 500.00
Total	$ 9,500.00

CHAPTER 17

Evaluating results

There are three main ways of measuring results. These are *output, outtake and outcome*.

Output

This is the most common way of measuring Public Relations (PR) results, though also the least meaningful. Output means media coverage. That is the coverage that results from, or is the output of, the planned PR activity.

Output can be measured in a variety of ways. The most basic is *circulation (reach)*. This means the number of people who potentially saw or heard the planned messages. It is arrived at by adding together the published circulation, viewing or listening figures for all the media in which coverage is secured. With a very successful campaign that secures a large amount of coverage this can result in a total figure that is greater than the whole population. As a measure it is rather coarse as it does not take any account of whether the coverage is good, bad or indifferent. Nor does it measure whether people actually took on board the messages or changed their behavior. However, it does have a value as a coarse measure particularly when compared with the results for similar sorts of activity by your own or by competitor organizations.

The circulation figure can be made to look even bigger when *readership* is taken in to account. Readership is the figure that shows how many people are estimated to read each copy of a newspaper or magazine. For example, the evening newspaper in your town may have a circulation of 200,000 including Mr Jones. However, Mr Jones, who reads the paper on the train, takes it home where it is read by three other members of the household, giving a readership for that particular copy of four people. It is not unusual for some papers in the United Kingdom to claim to have a readership three or four times larger than their actual circulation. As with circulation figures, readership proves nothing beyond the number of people who potentially saw the message you wanted to communicate. And of course it tells you nothing about the number of your potential target audience who might have seen the message. (Television and radio programs produce their own ratings figures which estimate their audiences.)

A better use of circulation and readership figures is to link them to *target audience figures*. For example, a newspaper may have a claimed readership of 750,000 but a reach of 250,000 amongst your target audience. Target audience reach gives a lower figure than circulation or readership, but a more meaningful one.

A further level of sophistication can be added by measuring how much of the coverage includes some or all of your planned *key messages*. This can be refined even further by measuring the *size and prominence of each piece*. For example, a piece of coverage that dominates the front page is likely to have far more impact than a small piece buried on page 32. Finally, you can compare your coverage with that of the *competition*, though obviously this increases the time and cost involved in evaluating your work.

The advantages of measuring by output are that it is relatively cheap, easy to do and readily understood. The disadvantages are that it does not really tell you what the PR actually achieved in terms of attitudinal or behavioral changes. It only tells you what has appeared. To find out about this you need to look at 'outtake'.

Outtake

This is concerned with what people take out from having heard or read your messages. It measures changes in attitude. For example, do people now believe, as you had planned, that you are a superior manufacturer? Have they changed their mind about the factory you are proposing to build? Are they willing to consider your offer next time they make a purchase?

The only way of finding this out is through research. What happens is that an expert researcher identifies a sample group of people who have been exposed to your PR messages. The researcher then asks them a series of questions to find out how far, if at all, they have been influenced by your PR. If, for example, 50 percent of the sample say they have been positively influenced then it is not unreasonable to conclude that 50 percent of all those exposed to your messages were influenced in the same way.

The advantage of this approach is that it gives a much clearer indication of whether the messages got through. However, it is not cheap. Indeed a true measure of what a PR campaign has achieved normally requires a preliminary benchmarking survey to find out what people think before the campaign and then later research to test the effect of the campaign. It is, therefore, often out of the reach of smaller companies, and fails the cost-benefit test for all but large PR campaigns. Moreover, this sort of research can never be totally accurate, first because it only looks at a sample not the whole target audience, and second because people are not totally honest when answering researchers' questions. For example, questions relating to sex, money and morality are notoriously tricky. Even when answering a computer-based questionnaire people like to look good. Admitting you are mean, promiscuous or immoral does not generally enhance people's self-esteem so they tend to be less honest than usual. Moreover by asking people questions you are obliging them to take an interest in something which may concern them very little: surveys of this kind have difficultly in establishing how strongly people feel about an issue.

> Perceptions are real. If you're playing to win they have to be favourable. Your ability to persuade people to listen to you, understand what you are saying, and support you will determine whether you win or lose.
>
> Lord Bell, Chairman of
> Chime Communications plc

Outcome

The most effective way of measuring a PR campaign is by looking at changes in behavior. This is called the outcome as it describes the outcome of your activity. The measurement of outcome is comparatively easy when PR is the only communication discipline at work and there are no other factors at work. Any increase in sales, calls to the help center, hits to the website, changes in voting intentions and so forth can be simply measured and put down to the PR campaign. Proof perfect that the PR has worked. You can even work out the cost per sale, enquiry or vote by dividing the cost of the PR campaign by the total response figure. However, this is all more difficult when there are other communication disciplines or other factors at work at the same time.

In these circumstances there are a number of things that can be done to try to clarify PR's contribution. For example, the PR activity can be timed to occur in the gaps between the advertising. Alternatively, PR can, if practical, be allocated different helpline or sales numbers or PO boxes, and also a different web address. In this way PR's contribution can be differentiated from other communication activity.

What is certain is that the evaluation of PR campaigns is fraught with problems, yet without proper evaluation of the effectiveness of campaigns PR cannot claim to be a measurable management discipline like other management disciplines. Moreover, measurement forces PR practitioners to be realistic about what they can achieve. Too often in the past the credibility and value of PR has been undermined by PR people making unrealistic claims about what is going to be achieved. And without the endorsement provided by measurement PR will always have difficulty claiming a place at the top table of the organizations that use it, or indeed significantly increasing its budgets. But despite this the proper evaluation of PR results remains something more talked about than practiced at the highest level. Why is this so?

There are at least *three barriers to the effective evaluation of PR:*
- Cost
- Confusion
- Containment

Cost

When PR is used as a part of the marketing mix it is usually the cheapest of all the marketing communication disciplines. An advertising campaign for a national company may well cost millions of dollars in terms of buying media space. The cost of evaluating results when set against this may seem quite small. For example, let us imagine that five million dollars is spent on advertising and the cost of evaluation is 100,000 dollars or two percent of the total. Now let us imagine that 100,000 dollars is spent on a PR campaign and that the cost of evaluation is 50,000 dollars. So the total cost of the evaluation is much less than for the advertising, but the cost as a percentage of the total is 50 percent. Rightly or wrongly many organizations would rather trust their judgment as to whether a campaign has worked rather than spend half as much again on evaluation. Ironically, PR's perceived cost effectiveness militates against it being properly measured.

Consequently, all too often, instead of measuring the actual effect of PR on the target audiences' attitudes people measure the effect of PR on the media – the "output." Whilst research evidence indicates that generally media coverage helps change peoples' attitudes this is a long way short of providing proof for each and every PR campaign. Without firm proof of results PR continues to struggle to earn the respect and budgets it deserves.

Confusion

Another problem that PR confronts when used as part of a marketing communication mix is confusion. By this we mean the confusion that exists over what part of the mix achieved what. For example, let us imagine that a company launching a small motorcycle carries out a marketing campaign that includes extensive PR in specialist and general media. The PR secures some excellent reviews of the motorcycle in key media. The PR also achieves the endorsement of a couple of leading celebrities who appear in photographs in lifestyle magazines and on TV riding the new bike. Within just three months sales are well ahead of target and the factory is working round the clock to meet the demand. The PR has surely been a huge success? Well, yes, probably.

The problem is that at the same time as the PR was going on there was a nationwide poster advertising campaign costing five million dollars. Market research shows that 80 percent of the target audience saw the advertising and liked it – only 20 percent of the audience said they had seen the PR generated media coverage. There was also a direct mail campaign which achieved a five per cent response rate (well above the average for direct mail). Finally, there was a sales promotion campaign in all key motorcycle retailers. The retailers with the sales promotion material sold twice as many bikes as the retailers without. You can probably see the problem. The other marketing disciplines have some hard data to prove their effectiveness. All the PR has is the coverage and a rather disappointing 20 percent recall rate.

In fact most research asking people where they saw information on something underreports the effects of PR. Indeed, it is not unusual for consumers to say they found out about a product through advertising when there has been no advertising! This is not because people are liars but because people give very little thought to their answers, particularly when they are being asked about something – quite often as they are rushing along the street – that happened a little while back. Answering with the word 'advertising' is much easier than saying 'media coverage' or 'editorial.'

So what role did PR play? Well the best way to find out would be to conduct the campaign without PR to see what happens. Of course this cannot be done – and ironically few would want to take the chance because most marketing people believe PR plays a very important role … they just find it hard to prove. (Some very big campaigns are trialled using a mix of different marketing techniques to see what works best, but first this is costly, and second it is not entirely accurate as the trials are usually conducted in different areas and one area is seldom very like another. The trial may, therefore, give a distorted picture.)

The likely reality is that PR played a very important role in our imaginary motorcycle company's fortunes. Without the positive media coverage would so many people have responded to the direct mail, thought positively about the advertising and bothered to go into a retailer to have a look at the new bike? The answer is almost definitely not.

Containment

As we will see in the chapter on crisis management, containing bad news and keeping stories out of the media or at least reducing the amount and tone of negative coverage can be a vital PR role. Indeed moderating bad coverage in a crisis situation is usually harder to achieve than getting some positive coverage in good times. But how do you measure that? How can you say how much bad coverage there would have been and how can you measure what the effect of the coverage, if it had appeared, would have been? The answer, of course, is that you cannot do so with any accuracy at all. What has to be used instead is judgment. A survey in the United Kingdom by Bell Pottinger and Henley Management College in 2004 of chief executives of top businesses found that the majority was convinced that PR was a valuable and important tool, but believed that it was not really possible to measure its true value.

Media analysis and evaluation

Despite the barriers to effective evaluation of PR results, the measurement of PR is on the increase and is becoming more sophisticated – particularly where it is the only communication discipline in play or when its effects can be isolated and examined separately. It is not perhaps surprising that a lot of PR measurement tends to focus on what is often seen as the heart and soul of PR, namely media coverage (including new media). Positive media coverage in itself does not prove a change in behavior or attitudes (nor is it necessarily the result of PR – not quite everything that appears in the media is the fruit of PR activity!) but it is likely to be a very strong indicator of success – that, after all, is an important reason why businesspeople pay for PR in the first place. After all, if something has appeared in the media it means that journalists think it is interesting and journalists are usually pretty good at knowing what their viewers and readers will find interesting. It is also simpler to measure media coverage than wider issues of the PR impact on outtake and outcomes.

In order to achieve this a new specialist media evaluation industry has emerged. In many countries there are now specialist firms that will not only monitor the media for you and send you copies of your coverage, be it in print, on-line or on air, but will also analyze it in term of audience reach, inclusion of key messages and in comparison to the competition. To do this they employ trained readers and a variety of sophisticated computer programs. Their reports can show changes over time, measure coverage in different media outlets, regions and countries, and even show how individual journalists report on a subject. Apart from the economies of scale and specialist expertise they offer these sorts of firms have one big advantage: their view is seen as objective. PR people measuring their own success are always likely to be a little suspect. International media evaluation firms include Carma International (www.carma.com), Echo Research (www.echoresearch.com) and Millward Brown Precis (www.mbprecis.com).[1]

Echo Research working for Airbus SAS: Evaluation of an international multi-market campaign

Airbus commissioned evaluation when it found that problems with its new A350 model were affecting its reputation. The monthly reports prepared by Echo Research highlighted the range of coverage Airbus was receiving in different countries and regions. In addition to examining volume and favorability of coverage there was competitor analysis of Boeing, and a tracking report of the impact of press releases and key messages. It helped identify the different reactions of the Asian and European media to suggestions that production of a new Airbus model should take place in China. This evaluation enabled Airbus to reshape its messages and contributed, for example, to a decision to enhance the then CEO's visibility.

Source: www.amecorg.com

Although such companies can analyze what has appeared in the media they cannot measure its effectiveness in delivering the message to the intended audience (let alone its impact on behavior), nor its financial value. Their professional readers and viewers have to act as substitutes for the real intended audience which, however careful the training, always presents a problem: a middle-aged male reader may not respond to something in the same way as a teenage girl, but ensuring an exact match between audience and professional readers would be prohibitively expensive. Another problem is that proper media evaluation takes time. If you are running a high-profile PR campaign those paying for it will be forming a far more instantaneous view of its success or failure based on glancing at TV or looking at the print media: the important role of what is called a "gut-feel" should not be overlooked.

Some media matter more than others – Indonesia

A study of the top print titles in Indonesia reveals that the best-read titles do not necessarily have the most loyal or engaged readers. It looked at how regularly readers picked up the top titles, how much they trusted the editorial and how likely they were to switch to rival titles. Kompas is Indonesia's highest-circulating newspaper and the most expensive for advertisers. But it scored lower than Bisnis Indonesia in its affinity with upscale male readers, according to the survey.

Top-circulating magazine Hidayah reaches 11 per cent of upper-class women, but has far lower reader loyalty than AyahBunda and Femina.

"The study allows us to go beyond the usual reach figures," said Rubin Suardi, business director of MindShare Indonesia. "Print is an increasingly important medium to reach upper class targets."

Source: PR Week

PR consultancies and in-house departments continue to measure their own effectiveness (not least because of the cost of external evaluation). One technique which is often used in-house (media evaluation companies tend to disdain it) measures *Advertising Value Equivalents* (AVE i.e. if you bought the space how much would it have cost you?). This technique is much criticized for being unscientific and like comparing apples with pears – surely a glowing one page editorial feature is worth a lot more than a one page ad and similarly a two word name check in a piece covering a range of competitors is worth a lot less than a strong one page advertisement? In practice editorial coverage, while offering the all-important advantage of third party endorsement, is usually far more nuanced than advertisements (which contain only what the people paying for them want to appear): the same story can contain a mixture of criticism, praise and neutral or irrelevant information, making it hard to assess its overall value. Despite this, in an attempt to simulate the greater value of editorial coverage the advertising equivalence value is sometimes multiplied by a factor of three or more. There is evidence that in the United Kingdom at least the use of this form of measurement is on the increase. Its advantages are that it is fairly easy to do – most media have what is called a *rate card* which tells you how much it costs to buy different size spaces for advertising – and advertising rates are figures that most marketing directors and Chief Executives are comfortable with. Indeed it represents the only quick, cheap and easy way of putting a monetary value on PR work. This is the language which business understands and is particularly important when marketing budgets are under pressure.

A further problem with media evaluation is that, while it may be the most used form of PR measurement, by definition it only applies to media relations work. This may be the heartland of PR, but excludes many other areas such as public affairs or internal communications. Proper evaluation here can be very difficult: in public affairs for example a whole host of factors may cause a change of government policy and it is very difficult to attribute it to the activities of an individual lobbyist – and next to impossible to prove it beyond doubt. Gauging the success of a lobbyist will probably forever remain a matter of judgment.

What is certain is that without an attempt at proper measurement PR will not secure a seat at an organization's top table. PR evaluation will remain an issue which preoccupies all parts of the PR industry but we do not predict any ready solution.

Summary

By using the simple Results Evaluation Grid below – when you have drawn up your objectives and have finalized your tactics and then again at the end of the campaign – you should be well on the way to having an effective evaluation policy (Table 17.1).

Table 17.1

Results evaluation grid		
OBJECTIVE	TARGET	RESULTS
OUTPUT: what PR has produced – coverage, readership, inclusion of key messages, equivalent advertising cost		
OUTTAKE: researched changes in attitude, acceptance/agreement with key messages		
OUTCOME: Changes in behavior – sales, enquiries, website hits, votes etc.		

CHAPTER 18

Crisis management

A real life crisis: the continuing story
of the Bhopal disaster

In 1984 what remains probably the world's worst industrial accident took place in Bhopal, India, at a pesticide plant belonging to Union Carbide, a large international company. At least 3,800 – and possibly many more – people were killed and many thousands injured. Warren Anderson, Union Carbide's Chairman and CEO, together with a technical team, immediately traveled to India to assist the government in dealing with the incident – the classic response in a crisis of this kind – but he was placed under house arrest and urged by the Indian government to leave the country within 24 hours.

Union Carbide organized a team of international medical experts, as well as supplies and equipment, to work with the local Bhopal medical community. Anderson testified before Congress in the USA. He stressed the UCC commitment to safety and promised to take actions to ensure that a similar incident "cannot happen again."

The reasons for the accident are unclear. There are suggestions of sabotage but also allegations that, as the *New York Times* put it, Bhopal was "result of operating errors, design flaws, maintenance failures, and training deficiencies."

Union Carbide is now owned by Dow Chemical which points out that it took over Union Carbide's shares more than 16 years after the tragedy, and 10 years after the settlement approved by the Indian Supreme Court. However, activists are not satisfied and the disaster continues to haunt Dow. A spoof website appeared, purporting to be Dow's own, detailing its responsibility for the accident, and an activist pretending to be a Dow spokesman appeared on BBC

$\rightarrow$

Worldwide television on the twentieth anniversary of the disaster promising compensation. Dow and its then PR consultancy, Burson-Marsteller, threatened legal action to close the website, but this led to negative coverage in the international media.

In 2006 Dow Chemical was reported to have hired the PR Golin Harris to run a global campaign. Dow said it wanted "stakeholders to better understand how its products, people and actions contribute to human progress."

Sources: www.prwatch.org, www.theyesmen.org, www.dow.com, www.bhopal.com

The final part of our section on strategy and planning concerns crisis management. Unlike the other areas of PR planning that we have looked at so far this is about reacting to rather than creating events. It can also be about the life and death of an organization. A badly managed crisis can see a company closed down, personal reputations destroyed and years of work undermined. A well-managed crisis on the other hand can not only avoid these hazards but can even, in the long term, enhance the reputation of the organization concerned. Crisis management matters.

A crisis is usually described as a time of great danger or difficulty. Events suddenly, and usually surprisingly, spiral out of control. Rumor and speculation are rife, the media are banging at the door demanding explanations, staff morale hits rock bottom, and former business friends no longer take your calls. The organization is now in panic. The boss has locked himself away in his office and is refusing to speak to the media. Investors are withdrawing their money. Journalists have met secretly with members of staff and are now printing anything they are told even though it is not true. Before long the organization has collapsed.

This sounds extreme and it is. But it is not impossible. It can and does happen. So what can you do to avoid crises? How can it be possible to avoid something that by definition is sudden and unexpected? The answer is planning.

Planning for a crisis

This may sound like a contradiction in terms but most crises are predictable. Fire, theft and fraud all happen. If they happen they could happen to you. Similarly products fail, accidents occur and employees sometimes behave very strangely to customers. We know these things happen because we have read about them, maybe even experienced them first hand. As a PR practitioner your task is to try and predict these crises and plan what you would do in the event of them actually happening.

There are six stages in planning for a crisis:

- Scenario mapping
- Response paper writing
- Audience identification
- Crisis team formation
- Staff training
- Crisis manual production

- *Scenario mapping*: The best way of mapping out possible crisis scenarios is to gather together a team of people representing each and every part of the organization and then, with them, trying to predict what sort of crisis could occur in each area. Figure 18.1 below shows a simple starting point for a scenario map.

Figure 18.1

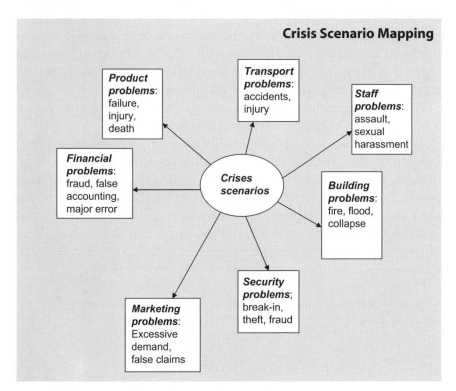

Clearly there are many more possible areas of risk depending on the nature of your business. In some cases simply identifying the risk will prompt immediate action to remove or greatly lessen the risk. For example, you may realize that your financial systems need tightening and that you need to improve the way you check references on the staff you hire. Or you may decide that you need to install a fire prevention sprinkler system in your factory or increase the firewalls around your computer to reduce the risk of identity theft. But whatever you do you can never eradicate risk altogether. This is why it is essential to develop a response paper for each potential scenario identified.

Response papers

A response paper is, as its name implies, a document that collects together all the relevant information on a scenario including the name and contact details of the person within the organization responsible for the area as well as the details of people or organizations that might back you up (allies and ambassadors) or people who might also be involved in the problem (suppliers, competitors and industry associations). It is vital that this information is ready to hand at the time of a crisis.

For example, imagine that you are representing a well-known food retailer and you have just been told that one of your lorries has crashed into a group of school children injuring four. The media are already speculating that the vehicle had not been serviced.

The example below (Table 18.1) shows an outline response paper for a crisis involving a serious vehicle accident.

By having a response paper readily to hand you can at least contain the wilder speculation and position your organization as one that has proper policies whilst you try to find out what really happened. A point to remember here is the fact that having policies does not mean they were followed properly so you should be careful not to claim that something could not have happened: it may have, but at least your company had taken reasonable measures to minimize the risk.

Having written a response paper for each scenario you now need to map out the audiences you are likely to need to contact in the event of a crisis.

Table18.1

Crisis response paper	
Response paper	
Scenario: accident or incident involving company vehicle **Summary position:** all our drivers licenses are checked before employment and are subject to regular spot checks. All vehicles are regularly serviced and replaced. **Vehicle replacement policy:** Every 100,000 to 150,000 miles or two years **Vehicle servicing intervals:** In accordance with manufacturers recommendations, usually every 6,000 miles	**Drivers duties:** Drivers must carry out weekly checks on fluid leaks, fan belt, tyres, brakes and windscreen etc. **Accident procedures:** any accidents involving injury to any person and / or third party must be reported to the police immediately etc. **Company vehicle expert:** Mr x + full 24-hour contact details **External experts/support:** This might be the garage or motoring organization that services the vehicles

Audience identification

A common mistake in a crisis is to only think about the media as they seem the most immediate threat to the reputation of your organization. In fact there are many other audiences all of whom can have a major impact on the future of your business.

Listed below are some of the key groups you may need to consider.

Internal audiences

- Senior management
- Customer facing staff (i.e. sales-force, service engineers, delivery staff, receptionists, security)
- Media facing staff
- Unions and works councils

Staff may quickly become demoralized without information and even worse may start feeding information or rumors to the media. All staff need to know if they are allowed to speak to the media: most should not be allowed to do so but should know how politely to refer or rebuff media advances. Those trained and approved to speak to the media need to be kept fully informed as the crisis develops.

External audiences

There are many external audiences who will be concerned. Investors will want to know what is happening to their money. Politicians, if it is a national crisis, may need information so they can make public statements and if there is a physical hazard local communities will need reassurance. Finally, there is of course the media, but more of that later. Some of the key groups are:

- Suppliers
- Customers
- Trade/Industry associations
- Investors, banks and financial analysts
- Local community
- Politicians and government officials (local and national)
- Media

For each of these groups it is also worth devising a plan as to how you would contact them in the event of a crisis. Will it be face to face, by phone or email? For staff do you have a system of cascade briefings whereby managers can brief their teams face to face? Who will be responsible for keeping the website up to date? All these questions are best answered in advance rather than at the time of the crisis when you will be under enormous pressure with a multitude of activities.

Crisis team formation

In the event of a crisis you are going to need a small team of people who can be freed up from their day to day work to focus on the crisis whilst the rest of the staff get on with the vital task of keeping the organization running as normally as possible. At the heart of the team should be a PR person and a member of senior management with decision-making powers. There will also be a need for a committee secretary to make sure that all the administration runs to plan. Depending on the nature of your business you may also need a legal and financial expert.

The crisis team should:

- approve all the response papers
- organize the relevant staff training
- decide who can talk to the media
- draw up the contact strategy
- produce the crisis manual

Once a crisis occurs the crisis team will need to co-opt the relevant company experts. These will be the people whose names you have already identified on the response papers.

The crisis committee can be called into session following a request by any committee member or by any agreed senior management members. For a small crisis it may only be necessary to liaise by phone. However, for a major crisis the committee will need to meet in person and a venue, with excellent communication facilities, should be identified at the planning stage.

The committee also needs to make sure that there is an extensive and up to date list of key people's round-the-clock contact details. Crises have an annoying way of happening outside normal working hours.

Once the committee is in session detailed notes should be taken, particularly of all media calls, noting the nature of the inquiry, the response given and all actions taken. It is vital to monitor not just the information going out but coming in as well.

Finally, do not forget that a crisis may run for 24-hours a day over several days. You will need to plan how you will staff your media handling. A press officer who has been working for 36 hours non-stop is liable to make mistakes.

Staff training

Agreeing who can talk to the media and ensuring they are properly trained in media interview techniques is an important part of the crisis committee's planning role and some tips on this are given later in this chapter.

Almost as important is the training of front line staff such as switchboard operators and receptionists. Unlike most other members of staff they are bound to have some dealings with key external audiences, not least the media. They need to be trained in how to do this and how to avoid some of the tricks that journalists play when trying to get or make a story.

One of the most effective ways of planning for a crisis is to simulate one. This can be done by creating an imaginary crisis scenario and then asking a few trusted members of staff to act as journalists. They call into the office asking for a comment on the crisis, the committee meets and the crisis plan swings in to action. A good simulation may run over several days. Whatever the scenario it gets staff used to thinking and working together in a crisis situation. This might seem like a major time commitment but is well worth it compared with the possibility of the plan failing when a real crisis happens.

Crisis manual

Finally, everything needs to be drawn together in a crisis manual. This should be available online to the committee members, but also needs to exist in hard copy format (imagine your computer system has failed!).

The manual should include:

- all the response papers
- contact details
- media handling tips
- media enquiry forms

It is best to present it in a ring binder file so that it is easy to update. It should also avoid technical jargon. Everyone from the security guard to the chief executive might have to use it at some point.

The manual should be updated at least once a year. People move on. You do not want to find on the day you have a chemical spillage that your chemicals expert left two years ago.

So now let us look at what actually happens when the crisis breaks.

Crisis management strategies

When a crisis happens there are a number of strategies that should be followed.

The first is to *quickly answer the key crisis questions*. There are always five basic questions that everyone wants to know the answer to. They are:

- *What happened and how?*
- *When did it happen?*
- *Why did it happen?*
- *Whose fault is it?*
- *What are you going to do about it?*

You may not be able to answer all these questions straight away, but as soon as is reasonably possible you should try to fill the information vacuum that occurs in these situations. Lack of information leads to speculation and speculation, in turn, leads to rumor. This can be disastrous. In the age of the Internet a rumor is half way round the world whilst the truth is still pulling its boots on. The key things to say are:

- What happened
- Why it happened
- What you are going to do about it *now* and to stop it happening again in the *future*
- That *you are sorry*

Organizations find saying sorry very difficult particularly as lawyers often warn that saying sorry is an admission of guilt. Saying sorry does not have to be an admission of guilt. For example, the injuries caused by your lorry crashing in to the school children may be the result of a manufacturers design fault and nothing to do with your servicing and maintenance. You will still be very sorry that one of your vehicles has caused injury. And if your organization is guilty of a mistake or failure there is no point in denying the fact. It is not just morally wrong but stupid. If it does not come out now that your organization was responsible it will just come out later and do you even more reputational harm. There is bound to be a disaffected member of staff who will find out and talk to the media or put it on the Internet.

A refusal to say sorry can make an organization look cold and heartless and do more damage to reputation than the original accident itself. Reputations take years to build but can be destroyed overnight.

The second crisis strategy is to try and *widen the issue and involve others*. For example, if the problem is not unique to your organization you may want to draw in the industry association. If the problem lies with a supplier you will obviously need their involvement. This is not passing the buck, though there is a reputational advantage in sharing the problem, but responsible behavior. If a problem is industry wide you alone cannot solve it. It is similar if a problem stems from a supplier's action.

The third strategy is to *recruit allies and ambassadors*. Think about who will support your claims to having proper policies and procedures? Who will vouch for your general good citizenship even when in a particular case your organizations actions have fallen below standard? At a time of crisis enemies and detractors are often easier to find than allies.

Big brands at risk: Pepsi and Coke under attack

The bigger you are the more likely you are to be attacked.

An Indian non-governmental organization called the Center for Science and Environment, claimed samples of Coca-Cola and Pepsi products contained harmful levels of pesticides.

The soft drink rivals combined vigorously to reject the claims and were backed by other soft drinks manufacturers who condemned the findings.

"Soft drinks are completely safe," the Indian Soft Drink Manufacturers Association (ISDMA) said in a statement. Independent tests ordered by the Indian government backed this view.

Some argued that the criticism of Coca-Cola and Pepsi was more about anti-Americanism than proper science. Whatever the case it cost the companies a lot of time and money to overcome the crisis.

Source: www.bbc.co.uk

Tips for media interviews

Journalists want the truth, but usually in the most sensational form possible. You also want to tell the truth, but probably do not know exactly what it is when the crisis first breaks and the media come on the phone or appear at your door.

This section gives some tips on handling press, radio and television interviews.

Controlling the situation

Before any interview try to identify:

- Who the journalist is and who they work for
- What they want to know
- The deadline for the information

Also try to get as much information to give as possible and try to prepare your answers to difficult questions that are likely to be asked.

If a journalist comes through unexpectedly, just say you are in a meeting but will get back to them as soon as possible. Then get the information you need and prepare your answers.

Whatever you do, *do not*:

- Get angry. However rude the journalist is it is not a personal attack.
- Try to be funny. Crises are not funny. Smiling is probably not a good idea either; it could make it look like you are not taking things seriously.
- Speak "off the record," in the belief that you have an agreement with the journalist not to use what you have said. There is no such thing as a true off-the-record agreement. Even if the journalist does not quote you directly, the only reason he or she is speaking to you is to gather material for the story he or she is preparing. Anything you say may be used, particularly in a crisis.
- Say "no comment." Journalists and the public think it means you are guilty. If you do not know what has happened, admit it but say you are trying to find out and when you will get back to them. Straightforward honesty is very endearing.

Whatever you do, *do*

- Show concern for those who have been affected by the crisis – this does not mean saying it was your fault.
- Forget *your* problems. Readers and viewers do not want to hear about you. They are interested in themselves or those who have been "harmed."

- Always be positive: never repeat the negative in a question.
- Use plain and simple language. It is important that everyone understands you.
- Make a few simple points phrased as simply and appealingly as possible.
- Correct anything that the interviewer says or implies that is inaccurate or damaging. Interrupt – politely but firmly – if necessary.

Tips for radio

- Do not move backwards and forwards or your voice will come and go.
- Avoid rustling papers, clicking your pen or jingling the money in your pocket. It sounds terrible on radio.
- Speak normally. It is up to the studio engineer to get the right level. Before you start you may be asked to say a few words "for level." Whatever you do, do not tell a joke about the crisis. Just say something mundane.
- If the interview is being recorded and you want to change something leave a short pause and then begin your statement again.
- Talk to the interviewer. Do not talk like you are addressing thousands. Speaking into the microphone is like speaking into the listener's ear.
- The audience cannot see you so express your feelings with your voice. Vary the tone and pitch.

Tips for TV

Appearance: Avoid extreme color contrasts, checks or stripes. Do not wear reactolite glasses, or they will turn into sunglasses under the lights and you will look like a gangster. Accept make-up if it is recommended. Check hair, tie, collar, shoulders. (It may also be a good idea to take a change of tie and/or shirt/top in case of any spills.)

Arrival: If it is a live broadcast from a studio, you will probably be asked to arrive well in advance and be taken to a waiting room for refreshments ("hospitality"). Avoid alcohol.

During the interview: Sit up straight, well back in your chair, arms resting on armrests or lap. Legs crossed. Always assume the camera is on you. Look at the interviewer, not at the camera. Ignore movement on the studio floor (e.g. by lighting or sound staff).

Ending: Thank the interviewer and stay in your seat looking at them until directed to leave.

Tips for press conferences

Press conferences have the advantage of enabling you to speak to a lot of journalists at once. However, they can turn into a feeding frenzy as one journalist's attack follows another. They are also open to hi-jacking by special interest groups or people with a grudge against the organization. It is better, if you can find the time, to deal with the media on a one to one basis.

If you do have to have a press conference make sure the room is comfortable and well ventilated (see Chapter 27 for details on events management). A hot and uncomfortable journalist is unlikely to be very sympathetic.

CHAPTER 19

Creating a socially responsible image

In many wealthy societies, where basic needs have been met, people now want and expect all kinds of businesses not just to be good but to do good. Sometimes they want this because it is much easier if someone can be good on their behalf rather than them having to make the effort, and sometimes they want it because they have seen that charities helped by business are often more efficient than large public sector bodies. And sometimes they want it because the only way to effect some kinds of change is through corporate action. The attempt of businesses in the developed world to respond to this is called *Corporate Social Responsibility*, or CSR. Perceptions of an organization's Corporate Social Responsibility can have an impact on all of its stakeholders. They can affect customers and potential customers, and shareholders and potential shareholders. A positive image can make it easier to recruit and retain good quality staff. And of course they can have an impact on how the media, public opinion, pressure groups and indeed government treat a business.

You must be the judge of how far this is true for businesses operating in your society, but you need to bear the following in mind. First, even if you feel that the circumstances outlined above are not yet fully applicable to your society, it is likely that things are heading that way: you need to be prepared. Second, you need to be aware that many overseas investors attracted to your country will have CSR as an important agenda item when they start to talk about doing business. Third, businesses operating and selling internationally – particularly in those markets where CSR is taken most seriously – need to think carefully about CSR issues: being seen to act responsibly can be a means of securing competitive advantage.

"Asian companies selling to overseas clients are finding they cannot win a contract without satisfying the other side that their treatment of the environment and their staff meets certain ethical standards." In some cases, multinationals seeking deals in Asia are having them granted only on government condition that they put "X" amount "back into the country" through community projects.

"Others are moving less out of necessity than fear; having seen the likes of Nike shamed in the international media for the working conditions of their Indonesian factory staff, they are devising policies and programs that can be used to give them a more friendly public face."

Source: PR Week

In such situations the job of the PR professional must be to help and guide the organization on, first, how to be good and, second, how to be seen to be good.

There are six guidelines that should be followed:
1. *Do more than the minimum*: When devising your crisis plan you should ensure as a minimum that your organization meets all the basic legal requirements. However, this is often not enough. Ask yourself and then the board would they be comfortable defending such a position on television. The answer is probably not. How can your organization go beyond the minimum and show itself to be a responsible and forward thinking company? Do more than is generally expected in your industry or sector. Try to have the best safety record, the most flexible working arrangements and the fairest recruitment strategies.

Chinese Lenovo beats American Apple on green credentials

In its latest "green ranking" of the world's biggest electronics companies, Greenpeace, the international environmental organization, placed China's Lenovo Group Ltd. at the top of the list, which is based on the recycling and toxic content policies of companies and is designed to get them to reduce waste. Previously Lenovo had come bottom of the list.

"It's a surprise that a Chinese firm which was bottom place in the first edition has climbed slowly to the top," said Zeina Alhajj, a toxics campaigner at Greenpeace.

Apple criticized the rating system and criteria used by Greenpeace, but that did not change the fact that Lenovo got the positive coverage whilst Apple was forced onto the back foot.

2. *Make staff aware*: Make sure that all your staff are aware of any charitable or social initiatives that the organization is involved in and try to create opportunities for them to be involved. Employees are, or at least should be, ambassadors for the business. They cannot be if they are unaware of what is being done and why. And do not just stop at the staff. Most organizations have an array of media at their disposal that they control, such as websites, newsletters and direct mail. Use them to tell customers, shareholders and other stakeholders what you are up to.

3. *Make it relevant*: Any social initiative or charitable involvement should be as relevant as possible to your business or more importantly your customers. That way it is more likely to have impact and be remembered.

4. *Be consistent*: Some companies change their charity arrangements annually. This makes it very difficult to achieve any real communications impact. The British retailer Tesco, which now operates internationally, operates a renowned Computers in Schools scheme which is famous in part because it has been around so long. Similarly, Pizza Express's support of the Venice in Peril Fund is admired and remembered by many.

5. *Be popular and topical*: The chairman may love golf but most people do not. Children, animals, the environment, other forms of sport and culture are all popular and topical issues and will generate far more coverage. This may seem cynical as there are many very deserving causes that are neither popular nor particularly topical. If your organization is prepared to be brave and different that is fine, but understand that it will take extra effort and money to gain a profile for such an activity.

6. *Be professional*: Doing good gives you no automatic right to media coverage. There are literally tens of thousands of charities and businesses working together at any given time. You will need to apply as much effort to the PR for these as you apply to the PR for your core business.

**Better Coffee, Better Life: a Hill and
Knowlton campaign in Thailand**

Working for their client, the global coffee giant Starbucks, the international PR consultancy Hill and Knowlton were charged with three tasks:

- Launching Starbucks' locally-grown Muan Jai coffee blend in Thailand.
- Positioning Starbucks as socially responsible.
- Educating people about Starbucks' "Commitment to Origin" programme which is designed to improve the lives of the coffee farmers.

Five per cent of the proceeds of Starbucks Muan Jai were allocated to the development of water systems and the provision of school materials for the Northern Thailand tribal community where the coffee is produced. Sales of the coffee – and production – soared.

Source: www.hillandknowlton.com

PART III

Skills

The skills required for Public Relations (PR) are many and various. They range from the ability to write press releases and talk to journalists through to the ability to present proposals to senior management, appear on television and organize attention-grabbing events. In fact few people are good at all these things, though most people in the course of a career in PR will need to show some skill at all of them. The exercise of PR skills is particularly sensitive to the prevailing cultural climate in different societies. You will always need to think carefully about the particular needs of the country or countries within which you are operating and adapt your approach accordingly.

In this part we offer guidance on all the key skills that a PR practitioner is likely to need. Inevitably in a book written for an audience from a broad range of countries covering the world's biggest continent some skills will be more important than others, depending on where the reader lives and works. Similarly, there will be cultural differences that are reflected in the execution of some of these skills. In a comparatively short book it is not possible to cover all of these differences. However, there is enough here to get the beginner started and help the experienced practitioner improve still further.

As we saw in the Part II on planning and strategy, what the media want is content that informs, entertains or educates. Like the writer or editor of a newspaper or the producer or director of a TV or radio program PR people need to have creative ideas.

CHAPTER 20

Dealing with the media

PR people deal with journalists all the time. Success comes from knowing your "enemy," which is the major reason why so many ex-journalists flourish in the Public Relations industry. Historically the love/hate relationship between PR people and journalists may not have been so evident in many Asian societies, but the growing dynamism of the region's media coupled to the rise of PR means that there are signs of change. Regardless of your background you need to understand how the media and journalists operate – and how to exploit that knowledge to your advantage.

Public Relations (PR) people are important players in what amounts to an information marketplace, and journalists are another group of players. They have to trade with each other – even if in most countries no actual money changes hands – and each wants something out of the bargain. PR people want the best possible coverage for their organizations, and journalists want a supply of the best quality news. These two desires are frequently in conflict. PR people often want coverage for things which the media do not deem newsworthy – if, for example, every new product received the kind of coverage in the media that PR people seek then we would read and hear about little else! On the other hand, what journalists reckon to be newsworthy is often exactly what PR people want to suppress or minimize: "bad news," stories about arguments, problems and even disasters.

Sometimes the crisis is real and the media interest is legitimate – there are clear dangers, failures or wrongdoings – but in other cases the public interest is less clear-cut. It could be that the journalist wants to reveal commercial secrets relating to a new product or service development, or publish disclosures about the private life of a senior figure in the organization. In such situations there is often a strong difference of opinion between the organization and the media. The latter will claim that what they are doing is legitimate journalism and in the public interest, while the organization will claim that they have some right to confidentiality for commercial or even personal privacy reasons.

To drive the best possible bargain in the information marketplace you need a thorough knowledge of how it operates and to keep up to date on market conditions. The following tips are designed to help you "trade" to advantage:

Newsworthiness

- What constitutes news is hard to pin down, but to be a successful PR person you have to have an intuitive sense for newsworthiness – seeing things the way a journalist or editor sees them. Remember that most of what comes to their attention on any given day is not covered – it is not considered news*worthy*. One famous saying is that when a dog bites a man it is not news, but when a man bites a dog it is. This sums up the idea that news is what is surprising, unusual and interesting: something new that people want to read about, hear about and see on TV.

- What constitutes news will also depend on the media organization concerned. Sometimes this is obvious. Local media will be interested in local angles – the implications of national events for the locality they serve, or the involvement of local people or organizations. Trade and specialist media will be concerned about what's relevant to their particular audience. But national media outlets will have their own characteristics and special interests. Popular newspapers, for example, will typically respond particularly well to human interest and celebrity-based stories, while the business journalists, especially in the more serious media, are extremely interested in anything with implications for the financial markets. This can be extended to individual journalists as – particularly in the case of those who are specialists – they have their own interests and prejudices.

- Most journalists have short memories, and most are general reporters, covering a wide variety of news and hence often coming fresh to each story they cover. This means that often they would not know very much about the background to the story: you have to bear this in mind and help them. As a result, with care, good news can often be announced more than once, in slightly different forms, giving you extra opportunities to get your message across.

- On the other hand, if the news is unwelcome, one of the best ways to play it down is to persuade journalists that it is old news, and that the story has already been covered.

Timing

- If you want maximum coverage for a story, "sell" it when news is in short supply. For example, government and commercial activity tends to slow down at weekends, when offices are closed and fewer announcements are made, but on Mondays newspapers still have to fill their pages and radio and television news has to fill its airtime. This has given rise to PR people offering "Sunday-for-Monday" stories, where they hope to benefit from the lack of competition for news space. Holiday periods can be similarly exploited, simply because there is less official and commercial news about.

- If, on the other hand, you are obliged to announce something which does not reflect well on your organization, wait until there is a glut of news – whether it is one event that is dominating the headlines or a series of big stories. Sometimes such stories can be anticipated, but at other times the opportunity arises on the spur of the moment, as an unforeseen event or disaster unfolds. If the media are preoccupied with such stories, and consider them more important than your announcement, then yours will receive less coverage than would otherwise be the case, or even none at all.

- All journalists are slaves to deadlines, the exact times when they have to submit their stories for publication or broadcast. It is hard to overestimate the importance of deadlines – after all, once a deadline is missed the news is useless to the journalist concerned – and so they have to be factored into a PR person's calculations. Obviously journalists would like to receive news well before their deadlines in order to give them time to prepare their stories. If the story you are selling is *not* major news then helping the journalist in this way is advisable: once they are close to their deadline they are less likely to bother with new material unless it is of the utmost importance. If the story is much bigger, the calculation is more complex. Sometimes it may be advantageous to give the media plenty of time to prepare their stories. At other times it can be beneficial to make your announcement right up against the deadline. This reflects the fact that the news media have to cover really major developments as soon as they occur – even to the point of newspapers publishing extra editions and broadcasters breaking into programs. If your story is big enough – and that means really big for the medium concerned – they will have to cover it in this way, and largely on your own terms, as they will have little time to seek alternative information or views.

To do all this effectively means being familiar with the media world, and being able to answer the following questions:

- What is being said about your organization in the media?
- What is being said about its rivals and competitors?
- What kind of coverage are issues which concern, or might concern, your organization getting (think back to the SLEPT analysis)?
- What kinds of journalists are involved in writing these stories? Knowing what they have said in the past can give you a good idea what they will say next. What are their characteristics and what opportunities and threats do they present?

Remember the media are moving targets. Media content, notions of what constitutes newsworthiness, and the ways in which stories are covered all evolve. Personalities change, altering editorial styles and approaches. Television and radio programs come and go. New magazines appear (and often disappear). Newspapers sprout new sections to reflect new specialist interests. Fresh kinds of journalism emerge in new media. To have a chance of hitting the target you have to keep studying it.

Trading news

The effectiveness of trading news very much depends on the balance of power between the PR person and the journalist. A small, little-known company will have little bargaining power with the mainstream media. Its aim is typically to secure any positive coverage it can for its products. Larger and more powerful organizations normally have more bargaining power because, as regular subjects of news stories, journalists are in constant need of their help. In the same way, "famous" journalists who are big names in the media have more bargaining power than junior reporters: they are much less reliant on PR people and if they express negative views they can carry considerable authority.

Offering "carrots" – the inducements PR people can offer journalists

- What journalists want from PR people is news, and what they want more than anything are "exclusives," news – as important as possible – which they can have first, before the rest of the media. Journalistic careers – and the fortunes of media outlets – can be built on exclusives, and so they are a valuable currency, indeed it is hard to overstate their importance. So exclusives, and even the hint of future exclusives, are both an inducement and a reward. They should be offered carefully, to journalists who are likely to use them in a way which serves the purposes of the PR person's organization.

- Journalists also like privileged access to organizations – for example, interviews with senior figures, briefings from experts, opportunities to film, or even simply a good relationship with PR people so that they remind them of forthcoming events or are particularly helpful when answering ordinary enquiries. Sometimes this assistance might involve an article written by a senior person at the organization – and almost invariably this is arranged and written by the PR person. This kind of general helpfulness is again a valuable commodity – without it a journalist's life can be very difficult – and it should be granted judiciously.

- Even if no money changes hands, journalists can often appreciate other perks of the job which PR people can offer them – which might range from lunch or entertainment through to free samples of goods or fully paid-for overseas trips (a particular feature of travel PR).

Using "sticks," or what to do with problem journalists

The measures below can usually be applied without any direct threat or action. Often only a hint is required. The position is well understood by most participants, and only in extreme cases is real action required.

- If, above all, journalists want exclusives, then denying them (or even threatening to deny them) exclusives can be an effective tactic. The same applies to other forms of help: even the implied threat of withholding it can be used to exert leverage.

- If the organization itself is insufficiently powerful to have this kind of bargaining power it may seek to purchase additional leverage by hiring a leading PR consultancy to work on its media relations. Journalists will immediately be aware that, in dealing with a large PR consultancy with a range of important clients, they are dealing with a potential source of many important stories, now and in the future.

Dealing with hostile stories

This is best undertaken as soon as possible, if possible before the story actually appears in the media.

- Complain to the media. PR people can complain about a story – ideally before it even appears – to the journalist concerned, but can also go over the journalist's head and complain to editors and senior management, or even the proprietor of the media organization. This can certainly place the journalist in an uncomfortable position, and many media organizations will hesitate if they face a barrage of high-level complaints.

- Such complaints can be backed up with threats. In addition to the "sticks" outlined above, the threat of legal action, typically for defamation or libel, is often employed. Even if they think they would win, media organizations fear the risk and costs and waste of time involved in long drawn out legal proceedings. Rival media organizations may be deterred from running the story if they are told about the threat of legal action. Other threats can include appealing to any relevant media regulatory bodies and withdrawing advertising.

- If bad news is anticipated, expectations can be managed by off-the-record briefings and leaks which give the media advance notice of what is happening. If the bad news is already known it is no longer really news: the sting is removed. Everyone – including journalists – immediately puts a news story into the context of what they already know. Indeed PR people working for highly successful organizations have to be particularly careful because the expectations are so high. If a company which was expected to make enormous profits made a very small profit it would be reported more negatively than a company which was expected to make very large losses and in fact only made a small loss.

- If the PR person is in a powerful enough position they can create and offer alternative news – decoy stories which serve to distract the media from the "bad news" story.

- If the story does appear, PR people should ensure that it is rebutted as quickly as possible. Challenging the facts in a story is aided by the speed with which journalists work. Very often news stories contain inaccuracies or errors, or rely on sources which might change their stories. Even if the central thrust of the story is correct, by undermining elements of it the PR person can weaken its overall credibility.

- Other tried-and-tested ways of undermining problem stories include the following:

   ○ Swiftly acknowledging and, where appropriate, apologizing for faults or errors, and thereby achieving "closure." Although this may seem a hard thing to do, once this is done the story often peters out, unless there are fresh ingredients, or the problem is too big for a simple apology to suffice. This technique can be combined with the following approaches.

   ○ Making the problem historic. If your organization faces criticism, make it clear that the criticisms relate to the past (which by definition they must) and make it clear that things have now changed for the better.

   ○ Attacking or discrediting the source of the story. Personalities are key ingredients in any news story and if they lack credibility or appear ridiculous anything they say is undermined. Sometimes you can supply an alternative source with equal or greater credibility who can contradict or undermine the negative story.

   ○ Pushing the problem away. Typically this involves setting up a review or inquiry, or commissioning a report. This is easily portrayed as a sensible and responsible course of action, but media coverage will normally die down while the review or report is undertaken. The delay can be used to prepare properly. Governments tend to be very keen on this sort of approach.

- o Accentuating the positive. Even in the most critical reports there are often positive aspects. Part of your job is to find them and give them plenty of emphasis. Make sure that anyone from your organization who is likely to speak to the media is fully briefed on the positive aspects. Even if they have to acknowledge or apologize for problems they can spend much longer talking about good news and what went right.

- o "Starving" the media. To keep going news stories need fresh fuel. If the organization at the center of the storm refuses to be drawn further and refuses interview bids the news often dies down (provided of course there are no further revelations from elsewhere).

- o Exploiting journalistic and media rivalries. Media outlets have a vested interest in undermining – where possible – their rivals' stories.

The points above all carry an important health warning. They depend on the amount of power you have and are seen to have – including your ability to control the news emerging from your organization (not always something that be guaranteed when things go wrong). Adopting a tough stance with journalists and media organizations may be necessary but inevitably stores up resentments which can come back to haunt you when you and your organization are vulnerable. Ultimately you will be judged on whether your approach was a legitimate one, in the interests of the organization and one which did not endanger or disadvantage the public, or whether your approach was simply designed to protect an organization that was seriously at fault and had avoided taking proper remedial action and responsibility for the alleged crisis or problem.

CHAPTER 21

Press releases

Press releases, media releases and press notices (they are just different words for the same thing) remain one of the cornerstones of media relations work. They are a well-established and recognized way by which organizations put across news and views to the media, and as such are usually expected by journalists when an important announcement is made. They have several advantages.

- They can be issued very quickly – almost instantaneously – and easily, through well-established distribution networks, in a format with which journalists are familiar. They are probably the cheapest way of making basic news and information publicly available, and are an accepted way of putting information on the record.

- They can be readily stored – for example, in online press rooms, making them available for journalists seeking background information. On websites they can be readily linked to additional background information, including downloadable pictures and even sound.

- You can control the exact content word-for-word – as you cannot if, for example, you ring a journalist and start a conversation.

- You can also control the timing when the press release is issued – to the minute.

- Press releases can be made available to all media organizations simultaneously, avoiding accusations of favoritism.

- They are one of the best-known Public Relations (PR) tools, known well beyond PR circles, and the people paying you and your non-PR colleagues will often expect them of you. But most press releases remain unused by the media – they are all too often just an attempt to show that something was being done about an organization's PR and to please paymasters and internal audiences!

While in some form press releases continue to play an important part in media relations work they also have drawbacks:

- They are used far too often and there are far too many of them: as mentioned, most are simply ignored or binned.
- By definition the information in a published press release is not exclusive – but exclusive material is what journalists prize above everything. Moreover, hard news is usually what an organization *does not* want the media to find out. All in all, surprisingly few of the biggest news stories start off as press releases.
- By the time everyone in the organization, including lawyers, has agreed to a press release the desire to be on the safe side means that the wording is often quite dull.

"Corporate top management officials should learn to refrain from interfering in the professional standards of media relations, by thrusting their views. They should learn not to convert the press release into an advertisement copy."

Source: K.Srinivasan, PResense

- If it is a big story the press release is only a starting point. Journalists will have additional questions as they try to develop their own angles and gather news and views from other sources. They will also want to interview people and photographers will want their own pictures.

Today press releases may appear more on online press offices on organizations' websites than on the printed page. The latter remains useful at press conferences or PR events when journalists are away from their screens. In such circumstances journalists still welcome pieces of paper. Whether the medium is electronic or paper the essence remains the same: press releases represent a way to try to get information and opinion reported – on *your* terms.

Top tips for writing press releases

- Always keep in mind the needs and wants of the immediate intended audience – busy journalists. What do they need to write the story?
- Shortness is a virtue: short words, short sentences, short paragraphs, short press releases.

- The headline and opening paragraph are most important: spend some time making them perfect!
- Your writing should be clear, simple and forceful. Press releases are not great literature or examples of fine writing.
- Avoid clichés, generalizations, superlatives – journalists will probably be skeptical if you say something is "unique" or "wonderful" and will not report it. It is better to explain *why* exactly it is unique or wonderful.

Figure 21.1

Press release template

Use your organization's headed news release paper – that way the journalist will immediately know from whom it is

Up at the top, the date – and perhaps a serial number to assist filing

A SIMPLE, SHORT, CLEAR HEADLINE

The opening paragraph is the most important one. It should be short and summarize the key elements of the story: **who** said or did something, **what** did they say or do, **why, where, when** and **how** did it happen (and, often, **how much** did it, or will it, cost).[1]

After reading this far a journalist will normally have decided whether the press release is of any interest. Journalists are busy people, working under pressure, who get bombarded with press releases. Most are discarded. So a strong headline and opening paragraph are VITAL.

The main text of the press release then follows, in descending order of importance: keep the main points to the fore, with background and explanation following up in the rear. In this press releases resemble news stories.

Journalists like to include direct quotes in their stories, and it is often a good idea to include them – perhaps your Chief Executive or someone similar commenting on the announcement – as it is a good, personalized way of getting across your organization's opinion about the events in the press release in a way which journalists appreciate. Put these quotes close to the beginning of the release, certainly on the first page. The quotes should use plain simple language – the sort of thing you would to say to someone, *not* the sort of thing you would write in an official report.

Notes for editors (at the end of the release, after the main text)

Despite what they are called, these are really intended for journalists, news editors and sub-editors. The news belongs in the main part of the press release, but this is the place to include supplementary information which might be helpful for anyone writing up the story. This often includes basic facts about your organization. Remember the journalist reading your release may know little about the subject and they have got to write a full story very quickly – try to imagine yourself in their situation!

Do not forget to include contact details (including how to get in touch outside office hours) – journalists may have questions or want to arrange an interview at any time of day or night. Highlight additional sources of relevant information, such as your website.

- Use key facts, figures and examples to make your announcement come to life. And paint pictures with words – saying something is as long as the Great Wall of China or the river Ganges is much more vivid than just giving its length in kilometers.

- Avoid in-house jargon (every organization has it!) and acronyms – keep in mind that you are writing for a busy journalist who probably would not be familiar with either. As someone who is being paid by an organization you may be under pressure to write things in a particular way, but remember, you are trying to communicate with people *beyond* the organization.

- Using quotes from key people in the organization or elsewhere (experts or celebrities who are endorsing the news in the press release) is often a good way of getting across opinions and making the press release usable. Try to make the quotes lively and as free from platitudes as possible.

- Always make sure that your press release has been cleared by everyone who needs to see it within your organization: you are issuing a very public announcement on its behalf, one that could have serious implications, including legal ones.

- Finally, make time to get together with someone else to read it through carefully before you issue it. Mistakes – even typos – are easy to make, particularly when you are working under pressure, and can be highly embarrassing – they can even become a minor news story in their own right.

Targeting and timing

Many press releases are issued in a single format for all media – the cheapest and easiest option. However, research backs up common-sense: if press releases are tailored to the particular needs and interests of particular media outlets they are much more likely to be used than a standard, one-size-fits-all version. Thus, for example, if adapted versions of the press release featuring local examples are sent to local media they are much more likely to meet their news criteria. Clearly targeting press releases in this way incurs costs and is potentially very expensive. PR people have to strike some balance in terms of cost/benefit, and judge how far to go down this route.

Clinique demonstrate how one story
can be used to interest a wide variety of markets:

Asian beauty survey

Clinique, the international cosmetics house, commissioned a survey that looked at the different views of beauty held by women around the world.

For example it asked if women were willing to go under the surgeons' knife.

The Koreans came top. At least half of them have had, or would consider, cosmetic surgery. However, only 3% of Indian women said they were willing to go under the knife.

In Japan 40% of women feel that money is no object if a skincare product is effective whilst Chinese women apparently do not feel pressurised to look more beautiful. Meanwhile, Indian women were most likely to rate (84%) women from their own country as the most beautiful.

Finally, the Chinese, Koreans and Indians are united in thinking that thick make-up on women is unattractive.

One story, but a lot of media angles for a variety of markets.

Source: The Malaysia Star Online

The best time to send a normal press release – something that is not exceptionally newsworthy but for which you want plenty of coverage – is as soon as possible after the appearance of the last edition or program. For example, a weekly magazine or newspaper that comes out on a Thursday will start planning its content for the next edition on that Thursday or first thing Friday morning. At that point they almost literally have a clean sheet of paper and will be more receptive to your news release than they will be the following Wednesday morning when most of their content has been decided on.

CHAPTER 22

Writing feature articles and opinion pieces

If you leaf through newspapers and magazines you will often find articles "written" by politicians, business leaders, even heads of NGOs. They have these people's names on them, and sometimes their photos, but who do you think actually writes them, and makes all the arrangements for them to appear? Yes, writing articles for the print media is another thing you can be called upon to do.

The opportunity to place articles in the print media can come from the media themselves, or it may be a matter of you taking the initiative. Sometimes newspapers will want an authoritative figure to write on an issue which concerns their readers, and you may want to seize this opportunity to state your organization's case. At other times, you may be the one making the call. As a Public Relations (PR) person employed by an organization, you are the nearest thing they have to a journalist. Your writing skills will therefore be in demand when it comes to putting together articles for the print media. You are also the person best placed to negotiate with the media.

Often such articles – particularly opinion pieces "written" by very senior people – are little read. This is largely because they are predictable and bland: senior people with heavy responsibilities are not free to be daring and use humor, gossip, speculative comments, controversy and colorful language in the way an ordinary newspaper columnist is. Your job is to make the article as lively and enticing as possible, but it will always be difficult: even if you are a better writer than your chief executive you are still bound by the same limitations. But even if the articles remain largely unread they often have an impact, not least because the newspaper can make a news story out of it or use it to stimulate debate. Your boss may also like the attention. It can also be a way of enhancing media relations: as a rule of thumb, the less important a media outlet is relative to your organization, the more flattered it will be to get an article from you. Like many good things it can be overdone. Indeed at one stage so many articles by the UK's former Prime Minister Tony Blair appeared in British local newspapers that he was sarcastically given an award as columnist of the year (the articles were in fact the work of a special unit of ex-journalists which was set up to produce them).

Top tips

- Make yourself fully familiar with the newspaper or magazine the article is going to appear in. What is its tone and style? What assumptions does it make about its readership? You have to bear this in mind as you prepare your article: there is no point adopting an abstract, academic approach if you want to appeal to the readers of a popular newspaper. Instead you might want to think about a strong human-interest story which would vividly illustrate your argument.

- But do not go overboard. The person for whom you are writing also has their own style and their own reputation to consider. You have to strike a balance – between the need to strike the right tone for the reader (and create a piece of writing which people will actually want to read) and the need not to embarrass your boss and undermine your organization: he or she simply cannot do all the things a newspaper might want him or her to do!

- Try to consider – as far as is possible – what context the article might appear in. Take into account other stories in the news, etc.

- Be wary of agreeing editorial changes after you have submitted the article. This can skew its meaning. Also be careful about the headline the newspaper chooses – that can have the same effect.

- If preparing an article does not appeal, you can always offer other options – for example, to answer readers' questions on an issue. These can be livelier than full-length articles.

CHAPTER 23

How to call a journalist

Journalists are very busy people. They can also be very rude, particularly to Public Relations (PR) people who phone them up and ramble on about things that are of no interest to them. So why bother to phone journalists? Why not just send them the press release and hope? Well, first because many journalists do not like press releases – some receive literally hundreds a day. Second, stories are about people, not pieces of paper. You cannot develop a relationship with a journalist if you never speak to them. And of course sometimes there is just no time to write and send out a press release. Even if you do send a release you may need to follow up with a phone call.

So how do you get the result you want and avoid annoying the journalist?

There are five steps to phone success. They are:

1. Prepare
2. Bridge
3. Taster
4. Offer
5. Close

Prepare

The first thing is to know the media you are contacting and know at least something about the journalist you are contacting – what did they last write about, what are their main interests? Why is this relevant to them?

Also think carefully about timing. For example, contact weeklies and monthlies a day or two after publication when they have a lot of empty space to fill, not the day before they go to print. Only contact morning papers in the morning when they are starting on the next edition. By the afternoon they will be too busy. The only exception to this rule should be if you have an amazing story. For most PR people this may only happen once in their life.

For TV and radio news and magazine programs it is generally best to contact the planning desk the day before possible broadcast.

Finally, plan what you are going to say.

Bridge

Establish a relationship between you and the journalist;

"I read your piece today on … and thought … ."

"You know the story you have been running on …"

"You remember the coverage last week about car servicing rip offs …"

NOT

"Did you get my press release?" How should they know? Why should they care?

Taster

As quickly as possible give the journalist the story or news hook. It is the one reason they have for bothering to speak to you.

"There is evidence that people are being ripped off by …"

"Our CEO thinks the civil servants have got it all wrong and is saying so in a major speech tonight."

"Our new safety suit could save two thousand lives a year …"

"One third of women say they prefer chocolate to kissing according to …"

NOT

"We are launching a new product"

Offer

Having given them the taster, get straight down to what you are offering. Tell them it is survey findings, an interview or a photo opportunity or whatever. Then ask when and how they want it (for example, post, email, courier) and make sure they get it.

Close

When you close you just confirm what has been agreed:

"So I will email it over to you by five this evening"
"Lord Morris will meet you at his club at midday tomorrow"
"We will deliver the safety suit to your office on Monday"
Keep everything as brief and to the point as possible. Email, the post or couriers are the place for lots of detail if that is required.

If they ask if they can have the story as an exclusive – which means no other media can use it – you will have to use your judgment. Is it better to get one big bit of coverage or several smaller bits? Can you give them an exclusive angle without giving them the whole story? These are judgments that can only be made at the time.

So remember:

Prepare
Bridge
Taster
Offer
Close

Exercise: Imagine you are approaching a journalist about an imaginary announcement by your organization. Prepare an outline of how you would go about this over the phone.

CHAPTER 24

Internal communications

A Customer Satisfaction study by the World of Titan retail chain in India revealed that one of the most important things when it comes to customer loyalty is frontline sales people. The message seems to be if you want happy customers you need well-trained and motivated staff.

Sandeep Kulhalli, business head of the retailing services group at Titan Industries said: "In a controlled environment we have seen the great impact trained frontline staff versus below average untrained staff make on the business ROI (return on investment)."

Source: The Financial Express

Internal communications, as we have already seen, is of growing importance in the Public Relations (PR) field. What exactly is the role of the PR practitioner? Well, all organizations have their own forms of communication – between staff and management (vertical) and between colleagues (horizontal) – and internal communications does not supplant these. Instead the term refers to planned and deliberate communication within the organization, undertaken by specialist staff who are not part of the normal vertical or horizontal information flows. As we have seen this role is increasingly undertaken by PR people.

There are a number of powerful arguments which you can advance for establishing a strong internal communications department:

- In an increasingly media saturated world internal communications is your organization's chance to correct or comment on messages which employees will be picking up anyway from the media. They might mention your organization, or they might involve issues with which your organization is concerned. For example, many types of business now want to reassure their employees that they have actively considered environmental concerns. If your organization is receiving favorable coverage in the media staff may not have seen it – but will be pleased to know: everyone likes to work for a successful organization (and it might even be a chance to blow the PR team's trumpet a bit!).

- Modern businesses need more and more highly qualified staff, and yet those staff can easily leave. Internal communications helps to inculcate new staff rapidly in organizational values and approaches. Good internal communications can therefore help to reduce staff turnover.

- Internal communications helps deal with other changes. People are less and less likely to work together at a single location, and restructuring and other changes happen and keep happening. Internal communications acts as a form of glue in scattered, fast changing organizations.

- Traditional manufacturing businesses made goods which represented the brand. Customers never got to see the people who made them. In the case of service industries however the person you deal with *is* the brand, and so making sure that, for example, call center staff properly represent the organization and its values is vital.

- Your competitors are probably investing in internal communications. If you do not you risk being left behind.

And there are also strong arguments for ensuring that it is run by PR people:

- PR people are uniquely qualified to bring to bear the skills outlined in the rest of this book and which are just as relevant to the practice of internal communications. They are experts in the art of communicating different messages to different audiences.

- PR people are the closest thing organizations have to in-house journalists. They can write material for newsletters and prepare material for in-house broadcasts.

- You cannot separate what employees hear about their organization from the media and other external sources from what they hear through internal communications. Any gap between the two will damage your credibility. PR people are best qualified to take account of what is being said in the outside world.

Top tips

As we have said, internal communications involves many of the same skills as other forms of PR work, but there are important differences. Internal communications is not about third party endorsement: *you* decide what appears in your own managed media, but the downside of that is that whatever is said does not bear the imprint of an independent journalist.

Modern organizations can control a full range of media aimed at their staff – print media, intranet sites and internal TV and radio stations. And it does not stop there. Internal communications can include posters, "direct mail," emails and text messages, speeches, meetings and other group activities, but also workers' entire physical environment: such things as buildings, art, furniture and interior decoration can be used to underline how an organization sees itself.

In designing an internal communications program it is likely that you will use a combination of media to put across messages. You will need to consider the following:

- What kind of message are you trying to deliver? Is it precise information about your organization and its activities, or is it more "mood music", designed to raise morale and give staff a flavor of what the organization stands for?

- To whom are you trying to deliver the message? All employees or particular categories of employees? Even if it is all employees then, in a large organization which employs a great variety of people, it is likely that you will need to consider addressing different people in different ways.

- What means are available to deliver the message? As we shall see, each medium has its strengths and weaknesses. Some may be completely inappropriate to your whole organization, or a portion of its workforce.

- As with all forms of communication, internal communications cost money. You will have to balance your ideal solution against what can be afforded.

Each medium has its strengths and weaknesses

- "Print media" such as newsletters can be relatively cheap to produce (although this will depend on their quality) and are good at conveying large amounts of detailed information, including facts and figures. They can also be relatively quick to produce, although the time taken for production and distribution means they can lag behind fast-moving events, particularly in a crisis. However, it is hard to ensure that staff read them properly and digest the information they contain. Typically people will read material which they feel is immediately relevant to them – for instance, if it affects their pay and conditions – and if it is very important personalized letters are often used, which offers a way of guaranteeing that people have at least been sent the information. It's much harder to get people actually to read about what the organization feels is important. To achieve this many organizations produce softer focus magazines or similar materials which use journalistic skills of the kind found in the mainstream independent media to make news and views about the organization more interesting and palatable. Key new staff can be introduced through interviews and profiles, questions from staff can be answered, staff letters published and competitions run.

- Internal TV and radio systems are relatively expensive and are suitable only for particular kinds of workforces – people who can be made to watch and listen alongside, or in intervals from, their work. They therefore tend to be used in particular kinds of large, well-funded organizations where the workforce is in a position to watch and listen. While both TV and radio can be excellent communications tools, compared with print media both are handicapped in terms of the amount of detail they can convey: a half-hour TV program typically contains fewer words than a large newspaper page. Moreover, broadcast media are of the moment: people can not readily refer back to them as they can to printed material – particularly important in the case of detailed information. It is also the case that some senior managers are not natural broadcasters – if they were they would not be in business – and their comments are better read than seen or heard. Looks can also matter. It is after all called tele*vision*. There is an old saying: 'they have a face for radio'!

- Intranet sites can offer both words and images, and have the added advantage of immediate interactivity: people can discuss issues, respond to questions, or indicate areas of particular interest to them. However, websites are expensive to set up and maintain (they have to be kept constantly up to date), although once in place they can be used by very large numbers of people without incurring significant additional costs. This makes them suitable for large organizations where staff by the nature of their work are well-equipped with computer facilities.

- In similar situations staff emails can play an important communications role, while mobile phones can be used to send short text messages.

- Talks and speeches can play an inspirational role. Although they are not a good way of passing on large amounts of information, by featuring key staff they personalize issues in a way which makes it hard for people to ignore or forget. For this reason direct contact of this kind will always play an important part in the "internal communications mix", particularly at times of change or organizational trauma. Speeches and talks can of course be interactive, with questions and debate, although if the organization wants to discuss – or appear to discuss – the issues at stake then seminars or other forms of discussion can be used. This kind of communication can merge with staff training.

- Other, "ambient" media can also play a crucial role, and, like speeches, are very hard to ignore. Posters and signs can convey and reiterate simple key messages. More subtly, art, uniforms, furniture, interior design and architecture can be used to reaffirm the organization's values and how it wants its employees to see themselves. Are they modernists embracing change, or traditionalists who place great value on past achievement? In practice most organizations are a combination of both, but the balance is different in terms of how they present themselves. One problem with such features of an organization is that many are not only expensive but take a long time to put in place: a company cannot simply find a new headquarters building which suits a new image. They are also so fundamental to the organization that PR input is bound to be limited.

In producing an organization's own media PR people need to display journalistic flair: they have to make their copy as attractive as possible. However, there are several stumbling blocks they have to look out for:

- Over-reliance on one method. As we have seen, they all have their drawbacks, and varying the medium can help to freshen up the message.
- Internal communications material can be boring. The essence of good, lively journalism is usually conflict and controversy, but the scope for this kind of thing in internal communications is very limited. Management pressures can add to this problem. Varying the approach and using different journalistic approaches – see above – can help to enliven the content.
- You should not contradict or usurp normal channels of communication within the organization, or you will arouse resentment. Remember that internal communications should supplement and not undermine management's role. Thus close collaboration with management is essential.
- Do not overdo it. Because you have a captive audience there is a danger of swamping employees with internal communications material. If you do so they will ignore and/or resent it and it will become counterproductive.

Example: Imagine an important message with far-reaching implications which needs to be conveyed to all staff within your chosen

Table 24.1

Internal message matrix		
Message	Internal audiences you would need to address, broken down according to the nature of the message	Appropriate media and communications tools

organization. On the basis of your knowledge of the organization consider how the message might be disseminated (Table 24.1).

Now imagine that as part of the above you have to write a short article for your organization's regular newsletter. Try drafting something appropriate, keeping your target audiences in mind.

CHAPTER 25

How to make an effective speech or presentation

Making a speech or presentation can be a nerve racking experience for even the most experienced person, but is something many PR people will have to do at some point in their careers, be it to an external audience or a group of senior managers or colleagues. In this chapter we have outlined top tips on how to plan, write and present your speech.

These are the key stages:

1. Planning
2. Structuring
3. Preparing
4. Speaking
5. Answering questions
6. Managing nerves

First let us look at planning.

Planning

- Find out about the audience and situation
- Define your purpose
- Focus your message
- Identify what you want the audience to gain and any action you want to follow

Research the audience and the situation

The audience is your consumer. Just as you do with any form of PR communication you need to understand them or you will not connect with them.

- What do they want?
- What are they like?
- What will turn them on?
- How long are you to speak?
- What audiovisual facilities are there?
- What are other speakers – if any – talking about?
- How will you be introduced?

How you are introduced is important. It establishes your credibility.

Define your purpose

What are your objectives? What do you want the audience to think, feel or do having heard your speech? What change do you want to occur? Is your purpose to:

(a) Inform (change their knowledge)
(b) Persuade/convince (change their attitudes or actions)
(c) Inspire (change their motivation)
(d) Debate/discuss (consider change)

The way you define your purpose will help define what action you want the audience to take following on from your presentation.

Focus your message

Your message is what people remember when they have forgotten all the detail. It is what they take away with them to act on or think and talk about.

The best speeches are built on the foundations of a simple message. Too many messages and people forget or misunderstand. Let us imagine that you are presenting to your bosses a proposal for an increase in PR budgets. You can probably think of lots of reasons why the budget should be increased. But if you present too many reasons the chances are they will not remember any of them. Try to focus on the three most important benefits to the audience of what you are proposing. In our imaginary case this might be that:

- We will get more and better media coverage
- We will then sell more products
- If we do not we will be overtaken by the competition

These are not only simple and memorable points but also provide a natural structure for your speech. It is also worth noting that these benefits include a carrot and stick – good things that will happen if we do and a bad thing that will happen if we do not. A mixture of the two is usually more effective than giving them all carrot or all stick.

Identify what the audience will gain and any action you want to follow

Listening to a speaker involves time and concentration so audiences want to know from the outset what is in it for them. So tell them up front what they will get out of your speech, whether by helping to solve a problem, gain some benefit, or offer some insight.

Amuse them if you can, as this will help keep their attention, but do not let an attempt to be humorous get in the way of your main message. Amusing the audience is just the icing on the cake.

If your purpose is to alter behavior be clear what it is you want them to do.

The action should be "doable" and easy to achieve.

Structuring

There are two basic approaches to structure:

- bottom up
- top down

With bottom up you work out all your points in rough and then look for a working principle to bind them together (work out the ribs and join them with a spine). If some of your points do not support the principle, drop them. The principle is more important than the points.

- With top down you choose the working principle … and then decide which points to hang off it. (Spine first then ribs.)

- The working principle is important. The audience's mind is a pattern seeking device. This means that audiences look for structure in what the speaker is saying.
- People remember messages not words. Using bullet points will help people focus on messages not words.

And very importantly have a three-point structure:

1. tell them what you are going to tell them
2. tell them
3. tell them what you told them

In other words, at the beginning tell them what your subject, structure and purpose is, then expand on each of those points and finally sum up by repeating the main points of your presentation.

Beginning: sell the speech

- Why you are credible
- Value (what is in it for them)
- Purpose (what you want them to think, feel or do)
- Structure (what the elements of your presentation are going to be)

Middle: the talk itself

A maximum of five points. Something along the lines below usually works:

- Situation/background
- Problem/opportunity
- Solution
- Benefit

End: a reminder of the key points and your message

- Summary of your case
- Call to action – if appropriate

Preparing

SPEAK – DO NOT READ

It is easier and usually more effective to speak from notes than to read a prepared text.

If your notes follow a clear structure and you are confident of your purpose and message you will not lose your way. Even better, speak from bullet points or visual aids.

You will be able to do the following:

- Look at and involve the audience
- Monitor the audience reaction
- Speak more naturally
- Seem more spontaneous and informal
- Spend less time preparing

Try to write your notes on thick card rather than paper as, if you are nervous, paper amplifies hand trembling – which, by the way, is perfectly normal.

Full text speeches are really only justified when you have to be incredibly careful about the words you use, for example, in legally or politically sensitive situations. Full text speeches are also usually very boring.

Limit the information and technical detail

No one can remember a lot of facts – least of all the audience. Try to stick to just the essential information needed to understand what you are saying. They can always ask questions at the end if they need more information.

Use signposts

Signposts stop people getting lost and also help slow you down if you are a fast talker.

Here are a few examples:

There are three arguments for this ….

Let us now look at why we took this decision.

Having outlined the problems I now want to look at the opportunities.

We are proposing a four-stage approach to the consumer called AIDA … Awareness, Interest, Desire, Action. First, I am going to tell you about awareness.

Use visual aids

Used well they do the following:

- Add clarity
- Add color
- Act as an aide-memoire for you

But do not do the following:

- Look at them rather than the audience
- Put too much information on them or they will be reading the slide not listening to you
- Reveal what you are going to say before you have said it
- Fail to differentiate key points from detail. Key points should be larger or at least a different color
- Have too many slides. We have all sat in presentations and seen on the screen, as the computer is loading, "1 of 49 slides." The heart sinks and attention slips away even before the speaker has begun

Rehearse

Ideally rehearse with someone. If that cannot be done use a tape recorder.
Remember that the actual length will be at least 10–20 percent longer than the rehearsed length.
When you rehearse think positively and picture yourself succeeding.

Persuasive speaking

According to the great Greek philosopher Aristotle there are three key elements to a great speech.

ETHOS, LOGOS, PATHOS

ETHOS – This is social/professional appeal – the appeal of reputation and personal merit. If the person introducing you has not established your credibility you must.

LOGOS – The appeal to reason. The logical and factual part of your speech.

PATHOS – The appeal to the heart and emotions. This offers the audience one or some of the following:

- Security/self preservation
- Status/prestige
- Pride of membership/belonging
- Power and control
- Fulfillment of aspirations

LOGOS without ETHOS or PATHOS is not much of a speech. ETHOS and PATHOS without LOGOS is usually just a crowd pleaser … . ask a successful politician! A really good speech will have all three.

Be graphic and enthusiastic

Use visual and oral examples and illustrations. Paint pictures in their mind. Be enthusiastic. Low energy speakers equal low energy audiences.

Benefits, not features

Benefits are what people are interested in. The "what it does," not the "what it is." For example:

A saucer is round and goes under a cup

Compared with

A saucer prevents hot tea spilling all over your lap when the cup jogs and gives you somewhere convenient to put your teaspoon.

Our computer has a 3mb memory

Compared with

Our computer will enable us to keep all our customer addresses so we can keep in touch with them

It is about what the audience will gain.

Carrot and stick

As mentioned earlier, it is often effective to express the negative consequences of the rejection of your case as well as the positive benefits of acceptance. Some of your audience will be more frightened of failure than attracted by the possibility of success – particularly if the possibility of success entails more work for them.

Give evidence

Turn your opinions into facts and use stories and case studies to prove your point. Tell them how organizations or experts they respect have done something similar or support the idea.

Set up the counter arguments and knock them down

Predict the barriers your audience will put up against your arguments and knock them down. For example, "some will say this is going to very expensive, but in fact by the end of year one we will have actually saved money."

Power pauses

Do not gabble. Speak slowly. People speak quickly because they are afraid that the audience will not want to listen, but no one can concentrate on someone who is speaking too fast. It is much better to say less more clearly. Remember silence is power. A pause gives emphasis.

Action

If you want people to change their behavior make clear what action should follow. Too often an audience is left feeling they ought to do something, but are not sure what or how.

Answering questions

- Look and sound pleased to receive them.
- Accentuate the positive even if the question is aggressive. If you are polite with an aggressive questioner the audience will be with you and against him or her.
- Thank the person for asking the question.
- If you are not sure you have understood the question ask them to clarify or rephrase the question yourself in a way that you are happy to answer.

- If you do not know the answer say so, but say you will find out or refer them to someone who can answer better than you.
- If the question is 'dangerous' do not hesitate to say this is not the forum. Or ask the questioner what they think the answer is.

Managing nerves

Being nervous before making a speech is normal. In fact actors say that the time they are really worried is when they stop feeling nerves before a show: then they know they will not give a top performance because it will lack energy. Nervous energy gives you the extra energy you need to project your personality and make your presence felt.

There are several ways you can limit your nerves.

Take a little exercise: Fear produces adrenalin which is meant to help us fight or run. With no one to fight and nowhere to run to the adrenalin dissipates itself through the trembling associated with nerves. So burn up the adrenalin by pacing up and down or even run on the spot.

Relax your muscles: If your muscles feel tight, gently lift and roll the shoulders and tighten and relax your facial muscles.

Take deep slow breaths: When we are nervous we tend to breathe too quickly. Inhale deeply and then breathe out slowly. This will not only reduce tension but help your voice.

Visualize success: Think positively. Imagine yourself succeeding.

In summary, use the nervous energy you feel to positive effect.

Summary

PLANNING

- Research the audience and the situation
- Define your purpose
- Focus your message
- Identify what the audience will gain (and what they should do)

STRUCTURING

- Bottom up or top down
- Beginning – sell the speech

- Middle – make your case
- End – sum up

PREPARING

- Speak, do not read (i.e. use notes not full text)
- Limit information and detail
- Use signposts
- Use visual aids
- Rehearse

SPEAKING

- ETHOS, LOGOS, PATHOS
- Be graphic and enthusiastic
- Sell benefits and features
- Use carrot and stick
- Give evidence
- Set up skittles and knock them down
- Be clear on the action you want

QUESTIONS

- Look and sound pleased to receive them
- Accentuate the positive
- Thank the questioner

This is an edited version of a copyright document written by Francis Hallawell.

CHAPTER 26

PR photography and images

In the United Kingdom a picture editor on a national newspaper may well see over two thousand images a day and yet probably only use thirty or so. Your photograph has to be very good to get into a national newspaper. However, there are now thousands of magazines and local newspapers as well as online media all desperate for content, particularly visual content. As the old saying goes "a picture's worth a thousand words," so it is well worth making the effort to create a great photograph or image. Here are our top ten tips.

- *Study the media*: Look at the magazines and newspapers you are targeting. What type of pictures do they use? Do they like conventional shots of smiling people sitting at desks or shaking hands, or do they like unusual shots with people in unconventional poses – for example standing on a fire escape and photographed from below. Draw up a list of what works. You will find that national newspapers are usually different from regional newspapers and consumer magazines are different from business magazines.

- *Make multiple images so the media can choose*: Given the different tastes of different media it makes sense to give them a choice of images. This will also mean that each picture editor has a better chance of having an exclusive picture rather than one that all his competitors are using.

- *Do not use advertising photographs*: Advertising photography belongs in advertisements. Press shots are much more natural. They are not as strongly lit and the people featured are not usually wearing make-up. You can normally tell the difference between advertising and a PR or press photograph by the fact that people in PR photographs look normal rather than perfect! Use a photographer who specializes in press and PR shots.

- *Do not over-brand*: As much as your boss may want you too, do not stick your company logo or message all over the picture. Most picture editors do not mind one logo in shot but more than that and they think it is starting to look like an advertisement and will not use it.

- *Provide vertical and horizontal shots*: Not all page layouts are the same, some need wide shots (often called landscape) and some need tall shots (often called portrait). Give the media a choice.

- *Write clear and concise captions*: Captions are very important. They should clearly and simply say what is in the photograph so that the picture editor, who may not even read your press release, knows what they are looking at. If the photograph is funny you might want to write a funny caption, but make sure you have put the hard facts about the story in first. If you are sending pictures by post it is also very important that the caption is very firmly attached to the photograph so it does not get lost.

- *Keep a portfolio of people, product and creative shots available on your website*: Increasingly the media expect to be able to go to your organization's website and find good photographs quickly. Make sure you keep the site updated. Your Chief Executive will not like it if the press use a photograph of his predecessor.

- *When organizing an event think about the photo opportunities at the planning stage*: Will there be enough space for photographers to move around and take shots from different angles? What is in the background ... you do not want to see an advertisement for a competitor over the shoulder of the celebrity you have hired at great expense. If it is out of doors do you have a contingency plan if it is raining?

- *Think about using graphs*: Not every story lends itself to photography but almost every story based on some kind of research lends itself to simple and easy to understand charts, graphs and diagrams. Have them available in camera-ready artwork form and downloadable.

- *Think about using cartoons*: A good cartoonist can be quite expensive for a small magazine or local newspaper and yet cartoons can enliven a page and add zest to a story. So if, for example, you have a story about lifestyles or families ask a cartoonist to draw something for you and then attach it to your story.

Earlier in the book we talked about creating a creative atmosphere. A good way to get you thinking creatively about photographs is to make a collage of great press photographs and stick it up on the office wall. Hopefully, over time, some of these pictures will be replaced with ones you helped create.

A photo-opportunity

The British entrepreneur Sir Richard Branson is known for his readiness to participate in eye-catching publicity stunts. When he launched Virgin Airways' flights to India he flew to New Delhi, donned the costume of an Indian prince, danced and then rode through the streets on an elephant. These colorful but appropriate images ensured massive amounts of coverage in the Indian media.

CHAPTER 27

How to plan and run events

The most important thing about an event is to be clear on what you are trying to achieve. The second most important thing is to have a clear theme or idea that will give the event purpose and engage the target audience in the desired way. The third thing is to attend to a mass of very important detail.

We have already looked in earlier chapters at deciding on objectives and how to create great ideas so in this chapter we are going to focus on the planning and administrative skills that are required to run a great event.

> M.A.C Cosmetics brand presented a cheque to the UNICEF China representative at a "star studded" event in Beijing as part of its commitment to supporting the "Unite for Children, Unite against Aids campaign".
>
> Apparently, M.A.C's donation will be used to "mobilize Youth Ambassadors and celebrities from China for the vital task of raising youth awareness."
>
> *Source*: Chinacsr.com

The first thing to do is create an initial event outline as shown in Table 27.1 below.

This can be updated and added to as the project progresses.

Once you have the answers to these questions you need to produce an estimated budget. This will not be too difficult if you have done events before, but if you have not then you will need to consider some of the factors outlined below before finalizing your budget.

Table 27.1

Event planner (overview)	
WHAT sort of event?	
WHY are we having the event?	
WHO are we targeting?	
WHEN is it going to happen?	
WHERE is it going to happen?	
HOW are we going to make it special?	

Organizing an event can seem very daunting so it is worth breaking it down in to manageable parts, each of which will need its own checklist and critical path analysis.

Some suggested key parts are:

- Budget
- Invitations
- The venue
- The event staging
- Performers
- The media
- Accommodation
- Transport
- Prizes/Awards
- Gifts/Goody bags

Budgets

Budgets have a tendency to be exceeded when it comes to events. The important thing is to try to cost as much as possible as accurately as possible from the outset so as to avoid nasty surprises. The budget pro forma below should help (Table 27.2),

Table 27.2

Budget pro forma			
Item	**Description**	**Budget/quote**	**Actual cost**
Invitations			
Venue			
Event staging			
Media			
Accommodation			
Transport			
Prizes/awards			
Gifts/goody bags			
Performers			
TOTAL			

Table 27.3

Venue checklist		
Item	**Description/Quantity**	**Status**
Catering: • Breakfast • Coffee/tea • Lunch • Bar • Tea • Dinner		
Seating plan and layout		
Signage • Branding/Logos • Directions		
Staging • Rostrum • Top table		
A/V equipment • Sound • Visual • Lighting • Stage		

Table 27.3   (Continued)

Item	Description/Quantity	Status
Parking • VIP • Others		
Media • Hospitality/ interview area • Invites		
Security • Front of house • Main room		
Rehearsal facilities		
On Arrival • Welcome • VIP welcome • Signing in • Cloakroom • Lavatories		

though each item will consist of many points. For example, the invitation needs to be designed, printed and posted, all of which costs money.

Having broken the event down into manageable parts, you now need to break down each part into its key components.

For example, a venue checklist might look something like this (Table 27.3).

This is not by any means a complete list. Moreover, this is just for the venue. Checklists also need to be done for all the key parts from performers through to transportation. It seems a daunting task and the first time you do an event it is, but once you have devised some checklists and developed a style of critical path analysis that you are happy with, it gets much easier.

CHAPTER 28

PR skills in the online world

"The things that keep me awake at night are the Internet and China."

Sir Martin Sorrell,
Chief Executive, WPP Group

There has been much debate as to whether the advent of email and the Internet has actually changed the sort of skills required to do Public Relations (PR), just added to the list of skills needed, or actually made very little real difference other than speeding up the pace at which things happen and messages are communicated.

There has also been much debate as to whether the problems that the online world poses PR practitioners outweigh the benefits.

The benefits of the online world are obvious and many:

- Faster, cheaper contact with the media
- The opportunity to reach very niche target audiences quickly and effectively
- Far more media in need of your PR content
- The opportunity for real two way communication with customers as well as journalists
- Rapid research providing consumer insights and trend tracking based on regular monitoring of relevant websites and blogs

However, there are problems with the online world as well as opportunities.

PR problems in the online world

> *"If bloggers are saying nasty things about you, you can indulge yourself in a campaign to try to improve what they are talking about. PR has become more important structurally as a result."*
> Sir Martin Sorrell, Chief
> Executive WPP Group.

Probably the biggest problem that the online world poses to PR is the ability of critics and dissatisfied customers to attack quickly, at any time and from anywhere. Before the advent of the online world PR (a) knew the enemy; (b) had some control over how their voice was heard; and, (c) had time to organize and plan a response to any criticism. Today the enemy can strike at almost any time and anywhere. Moreover, this potential for speedy surprise attacks on an organization has been coupled, in most societies, with a decline in deference to authority and trust in experts. People are now much more prepared to argue with authority, be it government or business, and will use the power and speed of the Internet to push their point home.

Some of the biggest threats to organizations are blogs. These are in effect online diaries or articles. The vast majority – and there are now an estimated thirty million plus blogs available online – are little more than gossip and chat amongst friends or like minded people and pose no threat, other than extreme boredom, to those who chance upon them. However, there is a relatively small but influential group of blogs written by people who see themselves as *"citizen journalists"* and either wish their views to be widely known (*renown*) or who wish to punish (*revenge*) an organization. Many writers of blogs care passionately about particular issues such as the environment or animal rights and raise points and publicize activity that mainstream media has yet to pick up on or has chosen not to cover. Overnight and without warning an organization can find itself all over cyberspace and then almost as quickly the subject of scrutiny by more conventional print and broadcast media.

Some blogs are specifically set up to attack particular organizations. Dell, the direct selling American computer corporation, was attacked for its poor service under the title "Dell Hell." Within no time at all the phrase grew in awareness until "Dell Hell" started ranking higher in search engines than "Dell" alone. Dell had to launch its own corporate blog to counter the criticisms.

MacDonald's, the fast-food eatery, continues to be the victim of blogs attacking it for everything from its environmental record to its treatment of animals and its working conditions.

What the online world has meant is that it is easier than ever to complain. An email is not only faster and less trouble to execute than a letter or phone call but also, once posted on the Internet, can be viewed globally. To make matters even worse, once on the Internet a complaint or an attack can linger and come up again and again.

Organizations have three options when it comes to deciding how to respond.

1. Listen in
2. Take part
3. Take cover

To *listen in* an organization needs to monitor what is being said. Fortunately thanks to the Internet this is easier than one might expect. Not only are there devices like Google blog search and Technorati[1] but, for bigger volumes, there is also specialist software. Media evaluation companies will also monitor online comment about your organization and its competitors in chat-rooms and elsewhere. Finally there are specialist consultancies such as Sigwatch[2] who will monitor groups that may impact on the organization.

Having listened in and found things it does not like on a blog or critic's website, an organization needs to decide whether to *take part* or *take cover*. As a general rule it is probably best not to respond as there is a danger of fanning the flames and making the story much bigger than it might otherwise have been. Many blog-gers are naturally anti anything they see as the establishment such as business and government and will take a response as an admis-sion of guilt and weakness and step up their criticism.

However, if the criticisms are valid the best response is firstly to correct the criticized shortcoming, and secondly to apologize. The biggest difficulty is when a complete untruth is published in a blog or on a critical website. Uncorrected the untruth may gain popular currency – there have, for example, been cases of products which have been accused of being carcinogenic when they are not. But trying to correct the untruth may just amplify the rumor and increase the damage caused by what might otherwise have been a very limited story. There can be no hard and fast advice in situations like these: you just have to weigh up the risks and make a judgment.

One way of handling persistent detractors is *try to get them onside*. This can be done by a mixture of flattery and dialogue. For example, an organization can offer to meet with a detractor which will make them feel important. Detractors can be consulted about new products or future plans and even offered new products to review. The difficulty is that some bloggers love such approaches whilst others feel insulted and believe that you are trying to corrupt them. Microsoft came under fire in late 2006 when its PR agency in America, Edelman's, sent laptop computers with the Windows Vista operating system to influential bloggers. Some protested at what they saw as an attempt at bribery. This sort of problem may lessen as the whole blogging culture becomes more established and more like traditional media. Indeed, some successful blogs are already forming themselves in to money-making enterprises, though this begs the question of whether blogs will lose their impact when they start to be seen and behave as other mainstream media.

As an extension of trying to get blog critics onside some organizations have tried to *join the blogosphere*. This is most commonly done by creating a corporate blog. One big advantage of a corporate blog is that it can greatly increase your search engine optimization. The danger with corporate blogs is that they end up looking like a boring corporate website rather than a real, personalized blog. This is more likely to offend critics still further than to win people over. The very essence of the blogosphere is its informality, frankness and openness. Running an effective corporate blog takes time – daily updates are usually necessary – and a willingness to show the skeletons in the company's cupboards. If you do a corporate blog you must be serious and honest about it.

The giant American retailer Wal-Mart ran into trouble when a pro-Wal-Mart blog purportedly created by a couple traveling across the States was revealed to be funded by "Working Families for Wal-Mart' (WFWM) a front group or organization set up to show Wal-Mart in a good light. Transparency is paramount for corporates trying to go head on in cyberspace.

At their best corporate blogs can be an extension of customer service, provide consumer insights, and even open up new areas of business. At their worst they can do far more harm than good. So before creating a corporate blog make sure you have a first rate online press office.

> **Tracking online discussions**
>
> International PR consultancy Edelman, working together with Shanghai online research consultancy CIC, has been tracking online healthcare and pharmaceutical discussions. Using specially designed software the research will look at different disease or treatment areas.
>
> The study reveals China's Internet users generated almost 1.5 million pharmaceutical and healthcare related messages between July and September 2006, primarily on blogs and bulletin boards.
>
> Helen Yan of Edelman says:
>
> "Healthcare and pharmaceutical companies in particular need to pay attention to these unsolicited online discussions. They provide an opportunity to gauge levels of understanding about important disease and treatment areas."
>
> *Source*: PR Week

Online press offices

Online press offices are important. Journalists (and bloggers) use them a lot. There are five main reasons why journalists use an organization's website. These are:

1. To find a contact (name and telephone, or email address)
2. To check basic facts (turnover, number of staff etc.), including past and present press releases
3. To see what angle or "spin" the organization puts on issues
4. To check financial information
5. To download photographs and other images

In fact an online press office can also be used as a direct means of providing media content by making available downloadable articles, features, photographs and even competitions.

It is also worth including in your online press office comment from external sources. For example, if you are selling medical products include quotes from, or links to, reports or institutions that have used and recommended your products. Similarly include examples of positive press coverage. A piece of positive coverage from one journalist is more likely to influence another journalist positively than all your persuasive PR words!

PR people and websites

Websites can be powerful communication tools, but all too often they fail to realize their potential. One reason is that often the guiding force is that of the technician and the web-designer, rather than that of PR people. Websites – particularly those belonging to big organizations – quickly grow too large and unwieldy for PR people to be able to exert full control. PR people, who are traditionally more familiar with print and broadcast media, also often lack the necessary expertise. Many parts of a huge website may be very specialized and require little PR attention, but nonetheless your role is to try to keep the focus on how the website can best communicate the messages that you want to send to your target audiences. You can help to establish clear guidelines, and can certainly maintain direct control of the electronic newsroom.

Problems and solutions

Major websites are usually designed using the latest technology available. Their designers view them on state of the art equipment using the best connections, but most of the actual users will not have the latest equipment. Websites can be a place to display technical wizardry, but that is usually not quite the same as your objective (although it may overlap). Instead your concern is message delivery to your selected audiences, who may not be so familiar with cutting edge web design and may not be so well equipped to use it. Will they, for example, like images which take a while to load on their computers?

Top tips on web design

Study what works First of all, have a look at a good range of websites which are trying to achieve something similar to what you are trying to do. Imagine you were one of their intended audiences. Then think what you can learn from their approach. What could you do better?

Keep it simple Think carefully about what appears on your web pages. People do not normally like reading huge amounts of text on screen – indeed unless it is very interesting or important (and especially relevant to them) they are unlikely even to want to scroll down. Instead, people typically like small amounts of information on a page – and then a clear way of clicking onto another page. This means that writing for the web involves thinking in three dimensions. Instead of people following the logical and familiar page sequence of a book or brochure, people will click on to whatever seems most interesting or relevant to them.

Make navigation easy Clear navigation is essential: users will not usually be familiar with your website and need to be able to find their way around. A good home page, a search function and site map are all useful. Keep your focus on what will be meaningful to your target audiences. The way your organization structures itself will usually be both unfamiliar and unimportant to outsiders: they will want to find the fastest route to the information and functionality they want, and navigation and contents lists should be designed with this in mind.

Avoid blandness and platitudes All too often websites are impersonal, bland and boring. Organizations which pride themselves on their personal touch find it deserts them on the world wide web. Senior people within the organization seldom have the time or inclination to give websites a personal touch, and much of the content is in the hands of technical or other specialist staff rather than PR people. Understandable legal and regulatory concerns can make the content very boring. The site can appear to be producer led, rather than reflecting the interests of its intended users. Blogs are often seen as a way round this, but as mentioned above these can also present problems. A website should be as interesting, and sometimes entertaining, as a newspaper or magazine – not as dull as a bad brochure.

Evaluation One of the beauties of using a website as a communications tool is that it enables you to monitor user activity much more easily than traditional media. Make sure that your web designers ensure that use of the site can be effectively monitored when you brief them. The crudest measure is the overall number of "hits" on your site, but you can go much further than that. To start with, how do they come to your site – if there are links to it on other sites, for example, how often are they used? Once there, which pages do people visit and in which order? How long do they spend on each page? How, if at all, do they respond to or interact with the site?

Interactivity One of the truly unique features of the world wide web (www) is the scope it offers for fast and easy interactivity. Users can email in comments, take part in live online discussions and many other activities readily and conveniently. By requiring people to submit their email addresses (as well as other data) you can also assemble a marketing database which can also be exploited very easily. This means that the www comes close to realizing a Public Relations ideal – two way communication between an organization and its publics.

Limitations However, it is also important not be bedazzled by new media, important though they are.

- Firstly, remember that, while the means of delivery is new, the content is still material which could be, and is, found on old media.

- Only a few websites could really be called mass media. The great majority of the millions of sites in the world are barely visited. One important difference of the www is that you have in some way to seek out a site from among those millions, and one of the main items of expenditure for website promoters has been traditional advertising and PR to market and promote their sites. Moreover use of new media is much more varied and individual than is the case with traditional media. The range is infinite and the way in which people view websites and blogs is intensely personal: it is much harder – although not impossible – to generate a shared experience which gets talked about via new media than is the case if something appears on the front page of a national newspaper or on a popular TV program. Indeed new media breakthroughs into popular consciousness often depend on them being taken up by old mass media outlets.

- Use of new media is patchy and changes swiftly. Even in some very wealthy societies large groups of people can find themselves on the wrong side of the digital divide, unable to access the Internet. Even when they can, they frequently find themselves left behind: those still relying on dial-up access will find themselves in a very different position to those with broadband access, and technology has advanced – and continues to advance – so quickly that computers which are only a few years old will no longer give people optimum experience of the www. PR people have to be careful about excessive reliance on new media: a lot depends on the audience.

Online press releases

Increasingly the press release is going online. The post, or snail mail as some call it, is on the way out. But does an online press release need to be different from its more traditional paper partner? The answer is basically no. An online release must have a great story up front, be well written and sent to the right people at the right time. Nothing new there. What does change is the ability to enhance the release with:

- click throughs and links to relevant background sources and references
- photographic and video attachments or links
- links to MP3 files, podcasts and computer graphics
- the opportunity for the journalist to communicate online with you in their own time

All of this should make the life of the client journalist who likes your press release much easier. However, there are several dangers inherent in the online release. First, there is a danger that because it is easier and cheaper to send an online release PR practitioners will be inclined to send more which will mean more of a journalists time being eaten up reading irrelevant press releases and more journalists becoming more and more frustrated with all PR people as a result. Emails are very easy to ignore. Second, there is the danger that the story gets lost in the technology and the attachments: journalists can have the same problems as the rest of us. Third, one cannot assume that all journalists will have constant access to the Internet – not all journalists manage to keep up with those at the top of their profession. The paper release remains a useful tool, particularly at press events: after all, it is much harder to scribble in the margins of an electronic release.

PART IV

The Future of Public Relations in Asia

"All research I've seen says that editorial publicity is better than paid-for publicity"

Sir Martin Sorrell,
Chief Executive of WPP Group.

Public Relations (PR) is a very young discipline in Asia, but one that is rapidly taking hold. As the quotation above from one of the key marketing services figures of our time underlines, PR offers specific advantages as a selling and promotional tool. This means it is on the threshold of very exciting opportunities, but will also have to face challenges and growing pains. Many of the trends we look at in this final section are specific to Asia, but PR is a global discipline and serves global clients, so we will also examine the impact of developments elsewhere.

CHAPTER 29

PR growth sectors

It is not hard to predict that almost all sectors of Public Relations (PR) work will surge ahead in most parts of Asia over coming decades. Indeed the process is well underway, with exceptionally high rates of growth in PR in China and India, to name but the two biggest countries. Many factors are at play.

Some of the most important ones relate to the changing business environment:

- A loosening of government controls over the economy in much of the region has led to the emergence of increasingly competitive markets, where companies need to try harder to convey a positive image and sell their products.
- At the same time growing prosperity and rapidly developing consumer markets offer new scope for domestic and overseas brands. As they establish themselves in the marketplace, they use PR alongside advertising.

A recent survey by Hill and Knowlton (China) Public Relations asked Chinese students what Chinese brands they thought were "cool." The white goods manufacturer Haier topped the list followed by computer giant Lenovo and sports goods manufacturer Li Ning. Notably all have benefited from a lot of very favorable PR.

Source: The China Business Review (online)

- New foreign investment creates further PR needs as newly arrived companies face a host of communication challenges in unfamiliar environments.

- Finally, as the Asian economies mature they need to promote their own brands in overseas markets, and here PR will also play a crucial role.

Underpinning much of the expansion in PR work are the fruits of economic growth. Maslow's hierarchy of needs can be seen in action, as basic physiological and security needs are increasingly met, and more emphasis is put on needs such as a sense of belonging, esteem and self-actualization. These new and often complex messages create communications needs which extend well beyond commerce. Modern governments make massive use of PR, as does the growing third sector, NGOs or charities, organizations which are particularly reliant on PR as they often exist solely to communicate a message.

Another important factor which affects all aspects of PR is the continued growth and diversification of the media, old and new. This expands the opportunities for media relations activity, but the sheer volume of media makes PR work increasingly demanding.

Government affairs or lobbying

Western PR firms setting up in Asia have all identified the enormous scope for public affairs or lobbying, and we predict strong growth in this area. In China, for example, a continuing legacy of strong government influence has placed a particular premium on public affairs: businesses need to know about government thinking on issues, and if they wish to influence government policy in any way they need to do it in a professional way. In many countries government affairs or lobbying has to be directed at regional or local authorities as well as national governments: how laws and regulations are implemented by regional or local government can vary considerably.

Healthcare

Healthcare PR is another area where we predict particularly rapid growth. Healthcare is a loose term which can embrace everything from the use of highly specialized PR techniques to promote pharmaceutical products to doctors, to the use of marketing PR to promote widely available personal products which provide health and hygiene benefits – from toothpastes to body lotions.

Marketing prescription drugs is often subject to regulations – hence the use of highly specialized techniques – but given the range and value of such products, and the amounts invested in research and development, it is a major area of PR work. The importance of regulations – products usually have to be approved and can subsequently be banned – means that public affairs and lobbying often plays an important part. Advances in healthcare across much of Asia will put an increasing premium on healthcare PR.

Non-prescription products are also the focus of intense PR activity as often they are unfamiliar and are designed to meet needs which hitherto were not apparent. As a result PR, alongside advertising, has to contribute to the process of public education about what these new products are, how they are used and the benefits that derive from their use.

Promoting toothpaste in China

Edelman, the international PR consultancy, was employed by Crest, a toothpaste brand which belongs to the multinational Proctor & Gamble. To promote the use of their product mothers were engaged as key decision makers with "Crest Van" school visits and road shows. The objective was to create an emotional bond with the brand as well as to communicate the functional benefits of Crest products.

www.edelman.com

Financial PR

As financial markets across Asia continue to develop, reflecting increased domestic and overseas investment in increasingly liberalized economic regimes, the flow of information upon which any marketplace depends will become evermore important. This will be reflected in the growing importance of financial and business media outlets.

Financial PR will grow in importance as companies seek to influence any reporting or comment which might impact on their standing in the market, and particularly their share price. This will spill over from financial media relations into investor relations of all kinds.

Continued economic development will also see more companies floated on stock exchanges and more mergers and acquisitions – all traditional focal points for financial PR work, and the source of high earnings for financial PR firms.

CHARLES WATSON, Group CEO, Financial Dynamics

"The sustainability of Asia's growth depends as much on the region's ability to access capital as on the economics of supply and demand. Across the region, hundreds of corporate entities seek to present the attractions of their businesses to the international investment community, in turn offering the financial comms industry one of its most exciting opportunities in years.

Since Financial Dynamics opened for business in Hong Kong last year, we have been overwhelmed with the opportunities. The Chinese IPO market is the most active in the world, with another $100bn of state-owned assets alone predicted to list on stock markets in the near term."

Source: PR Week, 2006

Technology PR

This PR specialization focuses on the particular needs of the information technology industry or "TMT" – technology, media and telecoms. The scope for this PR specialization in Asia is worth drawing attention to. Although there are many companies and consumers which already enjoy state of the art TMT facilities, the digital divide is very wide: many more people and businesses enjoy only very limited – if any – access to technologies which many of us now take for granted. The market may be growing swiftly, but the continuing introduction of new products and services imposes fresh demands. Marketing of TMT and education in their use and benefits will be a big task for PR.

PR for overseas markets

One exciting and sometimes new role for PR people across the region involves starting to think beyond domestic media and domestic audiences and beginning to devote more attention to overseas audiences, as Asia not only becomes ever more open to outside investment and businesspeople as well as leisure travel and students, but also starts to export more of its own branded products overseas. The growing role Asian countries play in world affairs means this has a government angle, as Asian governments try to reach and influence audiences in other countries through a process of what is sometimes called "public diplomacy." Often PR for distant audiences, in Europe, North America and elsewhere, will require collaboration with marketing services specialists from the countries concerned but it will still have to be controlled by people who are knowledgeable in the country of origin.

CHAPTER 30

Factors influencing growth

> *"The Chinese market place has far more demand than it has supply. It's very hard to find talented people who understand communications in China."*
>
> Paul Taaffe, Global CEO Hill & Knowlton

It's clear that the growing demand for Public Relations (PR) will ensure that the PR industry continues to grow in most parts of Asia. Indeed it will not only thrive in existing economic "hotspots" in India, China and elsewhere, but will increasingly spread into all parts of the Continent as PR becomes axiomatic for any sizeable organization. There is also already evidence in China that local PR firms have been managing to grow their businesses much faster than international firms, which still predominantly work for multinational clients. PR is no longer just an exotic import, but is growing naturally across Asia. However, developing a new business discipline imposes its own demands. We have outlined some below:

Training

A young, rapidly growing industry needs a trained workforce. That means more short courses which current employees can undertake to sharpen up particular skills, and more formal courses, offered by universities and colleges, leading to PR qualifications. This process can be swift: in the United Kingdom there were no university courses in PR 20 years ago and now there are dozens, both at undergraduate and postgraduate level.

Recruitment

The great surge in recruitment into PR will continue in many Asian countries: the industry has a long way to go before it matures. At present the profile of PR people is often very young, and what is gained in energy and enthusiasm is lost in terms of experience and perceived seniority. Although PR will probably remain a relatively youthful sector, we predict the following:

- A gradual ageing of the industry as early recruits mature;
- Ever higher standards of recruit, as the industry becomes better known and more popular and people throng to enter it;
- More mid-career recruits from related fields, especially journalism and, in the public affairs field, from politics; and
- Increased recruitment of people with PR qualifications who will thus have a head start in their careers.

Cultural differences will continue to require sensitive handling

A Ketchum Newscan survey found that many locally recruited staff in international PR firms in China felt frustrated or confused. They felt such PR firms did not properly root themselves in Chinese culture.

Source: Yujie He's University of Westminster MA thesis

Trade bodies

Trade bodies for the PR industry already exist in many Asian countries, but are still at a relatively early stage of development. They can play an important part in bringing together representatives from an industry which is otherwise very dispersed, scattered as it always will be across thousands of organizations of all kinds, from in-house teams to large and small consultancies. Trade associations of this kind can perform a wide range of functions: PR people can network, gather information, debate issues, promote good practice and ethical standards, promote and organize training and on occasion make representations on general PR industry issues to government and other external bodies. To get an idea of the range of functions they perform it is worth looking at the websites of the largest PR bodies, such as the Public Relations Society of America (www.prsa.org) and the UK's Chartered Institute of Public Relations (www.cipr.co.uk). We predict that trade associations will grow in size and importance across Asia because of the advantages they offer to many members, although for the reasons we describe in the chapter on ethics they will never become fully fledged professional bodies.

Publications and new media

Another force which binds the PR industry together is the trade press, providing news on PR-related issues, a forum for discussion and scope for industry-related advertising, including job vacancies, as well as staging conferences and training courses. The main international example is PR Week, available internationally at www.prweek.com. PR Week has representation in Asia through its sister title Media Asia, but trade publications in the PR field in Asia are in their infancy. Arguably separate trade publications are particularly important in the PR field because the industry's long-term tension with journalism means that it can receive inadequate or even hostile coverage in the mainstream media.

New media will also play an increasingly important part in the development of PR. Not only do the trade bodies and publications described above have active websites, but many other PR-related resources are available online, including the sites of PR consultancies. There is also a rapidly growing PR blogosphere, which has already spread across Asia.

Hand-in-hand with these developments will be the appearance of more books on Public Relations in Asia – to which this book is an early contribution. This will help to consolidate the PR industry's position, although, as we have said elsewhere, it would be a mistake to imagine the professional literature becoming comparable to that in fields like medicine or law.

All of this is not a one-way street. As PR comes under the spotlight it may face more scrutiny and undergo investigation and even attack. Journalists are naturally skeptical about PR and many people who view the activities of big companies with suspicion, including

NGO activists, look on PR with hostility. Critical books and articles which are specific to Asia may well appear, to match books such as *Toxic Sludge is Good For You? Lies, Damn Lies and the Public Relations Industry*.[1] The USA and, more recently, the United Kingdom have seen the emergence of critical websites: www.prwatch.org (set up by the authors of *Toxic Sludge*) and www.spinwatch.org Some of these attacks on PR already spill into issues which directly concern Asia, so visiting one or two of these sites and reading one or two books is well worthwhile. PR practitioners in Asia need to be prepared to deal with these challenges!

Combating a threat from environmental activism

In 2006 the Malaysian palm oil industry, under attack and under siege from green campaigners over its alleged threat to wildlife, began a major PR counter-offensive. Palm oil is used in many widely available food stuffs as well as other household products. The Malaysian Palm Oil Council is keen to stress its environmental credentials and the Malaysian Government's policy on protecting the country's forests.

Source: PR Week

The changing media environment

As we have already mentioned, PR practitioners need to keep a sharp eye on the media in all its manifestations. The media are always evolving, but there are particular changes which PR practitioners in Asia need to consider carefully as they have many implications for their work.

- In most Western societies, newspaper markets became saturated many decades ago, and, overall, newspaper circulations have been in slow decline for some time. This makes newspapers a less effective means of reaching audiences and has understandably led to increased emphasis on other media. While other media should certainly not be ignored, the continued growth in newspaper sales in many parts of Asia – at regional and local as well as national levels – mean they will remain more central to the PR effort for the time being.

- By the same token it is likely that the magazine sector will continue to develop very rapidly across Asia and offer great potential for PR. In addition to general, entertainment and lifestyle publications, there will be continued growth in specialist or trade magazines, covering particular interests, professions and business sectors. These are excellent media for well-targeted PR work.

- The volume of all media will tend to increase. Newspapers will have more pages and more supplements, magazines will be thicker, there will be more TV channels and radio stations, now regularly operating 24-hours a day seven days a week – and of course there will be infinite numbers of websites and blogs (even if there is some evidence that the first mass enthusiasm for blogging has passed). This creates opportunities and threats:

- First the opportunity. Creating media content is expensive, and media revenues and expenditure have not begun to catch up with the massive increase in media output. Put simply, slightly increased numbers of journalists have to produce massively increased amounts of content. Market liberalization also means that media workers operate under tighter cost constraints. This means that the media is becoming more reliant on PR, which offers content that is free at the point of delivery. That content will serve the interests of the PR people that supply it, but if they are clever the content will also be attractive and desirable for the media.

- The main threat is that with a hugely expanding media system it is harder to get noticed. There may be many TV channels but people only watch one at a time, and the same goes for print media outlets. Websites are so numerous that only a few could really be called "mass media". What has happened in the West, where this process of media fragmentation means that mass audiences are more difficult to reach, is overtaking Asia as well. It means PR people have to be more ingenious. Reaching audiences of all kinds is still possible, but becomes more time-consuming, more resource intensive and more costly (which creates another opportunity: the potential for more highly paid work for those PR people who can master the changing media environment).

- Another threat – hard to prove but possible – is that if the amount of PR content in the media becomes too great and too obvious it will become self-defeating. The special value of obtaining media coverage through PR was always third-party endorsement, but if it starts to look as though readers, viewers and listeners are no longer getting the independent view of a journalist PR could risk losing its unique selling proposition.

- A final "threat" is that in some societies the media's past – and present – reluctance to investigate and publish bad news about large and powerful organizations may disappear. Changing attitudes, growing dependence on advertising and increased competition for readers, listeners and viewers may well change news values and mean that PR people have to keep on their toes more. Moreover globalization means that all organizations with any kind of international profile or ambitions already have to face this threat in burgeoning international media.

- Globalization affects media just as much as other industries – and that affects PR in turn. Just because language, alongside images, may be the main common currency of the media does not mean that any media stop at national or linguistic borders. The worldwide nature of new media is well known, as is the CNN effect, matched now by many other international broadcasters. Powerful newspapers and magazines – *The Financial Times*, *The Wall Street Journal*, *The Economist*, *Newsweek*, to name a few – have become international in their reach. Their readership may not be a mass one, but it is an influential one, and in particular areas such as financial PR it may be crucial. The development of media of this kind, sometimes in collaboration with indigenous media, should be watched with care.

- Due regard must be paid to new media but over-excitement must be avoided. First, it should be remembered that while they offer new ways of reaching and interacting with people, all the things they do have been achievable by conventional media for a long time (albeit less cheaply, quickly or easily): new media are a means to an end, not an end in themselves. There have been a number of false dawns in the new media field already – in the West websites no longer have the cure-all reputation that they had in the early days of the world wide web (www), and even blogs are starting to look a little tired and over-used. While the development of new media in Asia may have further to go, Asian PR practitioners need to keep in mind why that is so. Although they and their associates may be familiar with new media, they need constantly to consider how true that is for the publics they need to reach. Affluent urban audiences for example may enjoy good access to the Internet, but how relevant are new media for reaching less sophisticated audiences? And, even as those on the wrong side of the digital divide start to catch up, the exceptionally fast pace of change in the new media field needs to be borne in mind.

Development of government PR

We predict that Asian governments of all kinds will become ever-greater users of PR, even if they prefer to call it by another name. In some countries PR techniques will be used for formal political campaigning – and increasingly this involves a continuous campaign, whereby no sooner is an election campaign won than attention starts to focus on the next election. In all countries however, regardless of their system of government, there will be greater need for communication between governments and governed. The exceptionally rapid rate of change – social, economic and technological – means that to avoid too great a divide opening up between the information haves and the information have-nots government will have to contribute to a lifelong process of public education. As governments respond to change they will develop new policies and programs which will have to be communicated to the relevant audiences, while staying attuned to public opinion: this is exactly the role PR is equipped to play.

The not-for-profit sector

As we have mentioned already, non-governmental organizations (NGOs) – charities and other campaigning organizations – have grown massively in numbers and importance in recent decades. Such organizations may avoid using the words "Public Relations," but for them it is in many ways more important than it is for business: even those charities which deliver services are heavily dependent on PR to raise funds. We predict several major trends in Asia:

- First, increased activity by international NGOs in Asia as they seek to further the causes they fight for in Asian countries both by applying external pressure on governments and business, and increasingly trying to mobilize domestic opinion on issues such as global warming and the environment.

- Second, the growth of domestic NGOs campaigning on a range of national and international issues. These will be major users of PR and recruiters of PR talent. Sometimes NGOs will be welcomed by government because of the assistance they provide in the process of public education (see above) and with social provision in a rapidly changing society.

- Third, a gearing up by government and business, including trade associations, to take on the challenge posed by powerful NGO campaigns. NGOs tend to enjoy considerable favor internationally, and often receive favorable treatment in the media, but sometimes threaten the interests of business and challenge government policy. This increasing problem requires skilful PR handling.

In 2007 a BBC environment correspondent concluded that activists in India were beating biotech companies and the government in the battle for public opinion over genetically modified food. As a result farmers have been burning their GM crops.

Source: www.bbc.co.uk

Ethics and corporate social responsibility

Ethical behavior and corporate social responsibility have become big talking points in the contemporary business world. In part this reflects increased pressure from activists and citizens whose concerns about issues may find more formal expression through NGOs and campaigning organizations – who in turn urge action on the part of governments. It is particularly evident in such issues as the environment and global warming, and fair trade and labor conditions in developing countries.

Although PR people are not specifically qualified to deal with these issues (which are often highly technical), and there is no reason to suppose that PR people are more or less ethical than others, PR people are nonetheless often in the front line when such issues come up, and indeed are often in charge of corporate social responsibility. This reflects the fact that they are more used to dealing with opinion-formers in the outside world than other employees, and have an understanding of how issues will be portrayed in the media and other courts of public opinion.

We predict this PR role will develop globally – not least in Asia. Domestic pressure will be one factor, as increasingly successful companies want to appear responsible, but globalization will bring external pressures to bear. Asian companies selling their own branded goods in international markets will become subject to the same pressures to demonstrate corporate social responsibility as existing international businesses, and concerns about ethical investment will rise up the agenda. All of this will involve more work for PR people.

At the same time PR will need to show that it is putting its own house in order. As we have seen, establishing and policing meaningful codes of practice for PR is always difficult, but the attempt must be made if the PR industry is to acquire a standing to match its size and growth rate.

The status of PR

The status of PR will rise across Asia as PR people – literally – mature and become a more accepted part of the worlds of business, politics and the not-for-profit sector. Their work will become more familiar and will become an accepted part of what every sizeable organization does. PR may feel hampered in its quest for a higher reputation by the fact that there's no real way of controlling entry to the industry and anyone can claim to be a PR person, but this is also an opportunity: the lack of restrictions means that PR in Asia can be dynamic and exceptionally responsive to needs. The ultimate test is the judgment of countless senior people in all areas who employ PR people. They do so more and more, and pay them more and more. That cannot be bad testimony to the power and importance of PR.

Glossary

Advertorial: An advertisement written and designed in the editorial style of the host medium.

AVEs – Advertising Value Equivalents: A method which measures media coverage by estimating how much it would have cost to buy the equivalent space for advertising (see p. 123).

B2B – Business to business: PR activity undertaken with the aim of helping a business communicate with other businesses.

B2C – Business to consumer: PR activity undertaken with the aim of helping a business reach consumers.

Brand: A product or company with a recognisable and distinctive identity as opposed to a commodity – for example rice or flour sold in plain, unmarked sacks – that has nothing that distinguishes it from the competition.

Citizen Journalist: A member of the public – as opposed to a trained, salaried journalist – who uses the Internet or blogs to report and commentate on current and business affairs. In a similar way members of the public also increasingly provide photographs or film of key events.

Community Relations: PR activity designed to promote relationships between organizations and the communities within which they are based.

Corporate Communications: Although this term is sometimes used interchangeably with PR, properly used it refers to those aspects of PR which focus on the overall reputation of the organization, rather than, for example, day-to-day marketing objectives.

Critical Path Analysis: A plan of action that determines the optimum sequence in which actions should be undertaken for maximum effectiveness.

CSR – Corporate Social Responsibility: Refers to the increasingly popular idea that businesses have a range of social and environmental responsibilities – to their employees, suppliers, local communities and wider society – and must not only act on these concerns but be seen to act in an accountable way. PR people often play a key role in CSR.

E-PR: Another name for online PR activity.

FMCG – Fast Moving Consumer Goods (sometimes called consumer packaged goods): Items which are replaced regularly and hence have a quick turnover. Typically they are relatively cheap. Examples include soap, toothpaste, shaving products and detergents. Global companies such as Proctor & Gamble and Unilever produce a wide range of FMCGs.

Front groups: Organizations formed by businesses to mimic NGOs and hence counter NGO campaigns which are seen as threatening their business interests (see p. 27).

Goody Bag: A bag of gifts given to journalists by the host organization after a press conference or press event. Goody bags are also often given to celebrities and key opinion formers after a PR organized event.

Horizontal media: Media outlets which cover a wide range of subjects, in contrast to vertical media (see below). Most daily newspapers are horizontal in character.

Integrated Marketing Communications: The bringing together of all marketing disciplines, including PR, advertising and sales promotion, in a coordinated way (see p. 17). Other relevant terms are "**marcoms**," short for "marketing communications" and "**the marketing mix**." PR used for this purpose is often referred to as **marketing PR**.

In-house: Term used to describe PR work undertaken within an organization by its own employees – typically members of its PR department – as opposed to consultancy or agency work.

Internal Communication: Communication targeting the staff of an organization rather than its customers or other stakeholders. Also called **Employee Communication**, **Employer Branding** or, particularly in times of transition, **Change Management**.

Intranet: An online computer-based communication system or special website only available to those working within an organization.

IPOs – Initial Public Offerings: The first sale of a business's shares on the financial markets, an occasion which typically requires a great deal of financial PR work.

Lobbying: Any activity designed to influence the actions of government or other bodies which wield law-making, regulatory or similar powers.

Maslow's Hierarchy of Needs: A theory that says societies develop through a number of stages from security, through socialization, to self-esteem and finally self-actualization.

Mass Markets: Markets where the product or service is widely available and affordable.

Mass Media: A term used to describe generally available and widely used media such as television, radio and popular newspapers.

Media Monitoring: Examining all relevant media for relevant coverage – of the organization itself, of its competitors or of relevant issues. Typically this activity, which can be very time consuming, is undertaken by specialist companies which can provide newspaper and magazine cuttings and transcripts or recordings of broadcast material.

M&A – Mergers and Acquisitions: When companies join together or take over other businesses. This forms the basis of a large proportion of financial PR work.

NGOs – Non-governmental organizations: Also known as not-for-profit organizations or even sometimes as the "third sector." NGOs are distinct from business and government and include charities and campaigning organizations, such as Greenpeace and Amnesty International, as well as many thousands of less well-known ones.

Online Press Office: Facilities for the press, such as press releases and photographs, made available by an organization, via the Internet.

Social Networks: Commercially hosted Internet-based services that allows online interaction between people with shared social interests. Prime examples are My Space and You Tube.

Spin: A pejorative term used to describe PR when it is seen to have been used to present a very partial view of the truth. People who undertake such work are called **Spin Doctors**.

Stakeholders: Anyone with an interest in an organization – for example, its shareholders, employees, customers, suppliers, or the local community.

Third party endorsement: The concept of an independent person offering a view on something about which someone may make a decision. In the case of PR the "third party" is the journalist and the media organization for which he or she works. Their independent "endorsement" of, for example, a new product is considered to be worth more than the equivalent amount of paid-for advertising.

Vertical media: Specialist media with a relatively narrow focus – they include, for example, trade magazines which are concerned with a particular business sector or profession and consumer magazines focusing on particular hobbies and interests such as sport or fashion.

White goods: Household appliances such as fridges and washing machines. These are much more expensive than FMCGs (see above) but are replaced much more rarely.

Notes

4 PR and integrated marketing communications

1. A useful definition of advertising by the UK's Advertising Association is as follows:
   Advertisements are messages, paid for by those who send them, intended to inform or influence people who receive them

5 PR sectors and specialisms

1. www.brunswickgroup.com
2. www.edelman.com

8 Public Relations ethics

1. www.ipra.org/aboutipra/aboutipra.htm
2. www.prsa.org
3. www.prsa.org

10 POSTAR, a PR planning aid

1. POSTAR is adapted from P R Smith's SOSTAC planning model – www.prsmith.org

11 Objectives

1. A method developed by Peter Drucker.

17 Evaluating results

1. Useful background is available on the media evaluation industry's trade association website, http://www.amecorg.com/

21   Press releases

1. I keep six honest serving men
    (They taught me all I knew)
    Their names are And How and Where and Who
    What and Why and When

                                Rudyard Kipling, journalist and poet.

28   PR skills in the online world

1. http://technorati.com/
2. http://www.sigwatch.com/

30   Factors influencing growth

1. For details, see Further Reading.

Further reading, websites and sources of information

Few books have been written about Public Relations (PR) in Asia, but the following, mainly British and American, books may be of use:

Sharon Beder, *Global Spin. The Corporate Assault on Environmentalism*, Green Books, 1997

Mark Borkowski, *Improperganda: The Art of the Publicity Stunt*, Vision On, 2000

Sean Brierley, *The Advertising Handbook*, Routledge, 2002

Hugh Culbertson and Ni Chen (eds), *International Public Relations: A Comparative Analysis*, Lea's Communication Series, 1996

Stuart Cutlip, *The Unseen Power: Public Relations, A History*, Lawrence Erlbaum, 1996

Gary Davies (ed.), *Corporate Reputation and Competitiveness*, Routledge, 2002

Stuart Ewen, *PR! A Social History of Spin*, Basic Books, 1994

Chris Frill, *Marketing Communications: Contexts, contents and strategies*, Prentice Hall, 1999

James Grunig (ed.), *Excellence in Public Relations and Communication Management*, Lawrence Erlbaum, 1992

Shirley Harrison, *Public Relations: An Introduction*, Thomson Learning, 2000

Mark Hollingsworth, *The Ultimate Spin Doctor: The Life and Fast Times of Tim Bell*, Coronet, 1997

Robert Jackall and Janice Hirota, *Image Makers: Advertising, Public Relations and the Ethos of Advocacy*, University of Chicago Press, 2000

Michael Kunczik, *Images of Nations and International Public Relations*, Lawrence Erlbaum, 1996

Philip Kitchen, *Public Relations: Principles and Practice*, Thomson Learning, 1997

Brian McNair, *An Introduction to Political Communication*, Routledge, 1999

Kevin Moloney, *Rethinking Public Relations: The Spin and the Substance*, Routledge, 2006

Michael Morley, *How to Manage Your Global Reputation*, Macmillan, 1998

Wally Olins, *On Brand*, Thames and Hudson, 2003

Al and Laura Ries, *The Fall of Advertising and the Rise of PR*, Collins, 2002

John Stauber and Sheldon Rampton, *Toxic Sludge Is Good For You! Lies, Damn Lies and the Public Relations Industry*, Robinson, 2004

Alison Theaker (ed.), *The Public Relations Handbook*, Routledge, 2001

The UK's Chartered Institute of Public Relations (CIPR) also produces a growing series of practical textbooks on aspects of PR in conjunction with the publisher Kogan Page. Up to date details are available on the CIPR's website at http://www.cipr.co.uk/Products/productsframeset.htm

Key international marketing services groups

(These sites include links to the large PR and advertising firms which make up these groups)

Havas: www.havas.com
Interpublic: www.interpublic.com
Omnicom: www.omnicomgroup.com
Publicis: www.publicis.com
WPP: www.wpp.com

The world's largest independent PR consultancy, Edelman, is also active in Asia and has a useful website: www.edelman.com

Activism and international corporate social responsibility issues

www.corporate-accountability.org
www.sigwatch.com

Public relations organizations

International

Association for the Measurement and Evaluation of Communication: www.amecorg.com
Global Alliance for Public Relations and Communication Management: www.globalpr.org
International Association of Business Communicators: www.iabc.com
International Communications Consultancy Organization: www.iccopr.com
International Public Relations Association: www.ipra.org

Regional

China International Public Relation Association: www.cipra.org.cn
Council of Public Relations Firms of Hong Kong: www.cprfhk.org
The Public Relations Society of Indonesia: www.pr-society.or.id
Public Relations Consultants Association of India: www.prcai.org
Institute of Public Relations Singapore: www.iprs.org.sg

Trade publication

PR Week is the main international trade publication: www.prweek.com. It publishes the following in Asia: www.brandrepublic.com/mediaasia/ and www.brandrepublic.com/asia

Some examples of PR-related blogs

www.eok.net
www.indiapr.blogspot.com
www.strumpette.com
http://news.imagethief.com/blogs/china/
http://www.blogworks.in/blog/
http://thepr2.0universe.com/
http://sosaidthe.org/
http://www.forimmediaterelease.biz/
http://www.globalprblogweek.com/

Critical websites

www.prwatch.org
www.spinwatch.org

About the authors

Trevor Morris BA Hons, FRSA

Trevor Morris is Visiting Professor in Public Relations at Westminster University and a business consultant and mentor. He was formerly the high profile CEO of Chime Public Relations, Europe's biggest PR group. PR week recently described him as "one of the most influential people in PR."

As an entrepreneurial businessman Trevor shaped and led the management buyout of QBO, a top UK PR consultancy, and then grew the business to achieve margins of over 30 percent before selling it to Chime plc in November 2000.

As a public relations consultant he led campaigns from crisis management to brand building and public information for blue chip commercial and government clients.

Former colleagues range from Lord Tim Bell (former Prime Minister Lady Thatcher's favorite PR man), David Hill (former Prime Minister Tony Blair's press advisor) and Rosie Boycott (journalist and broadcaster) through to Sophie Rhys-Jones (the Countess of Wessex, the wife of Prince Edward).

He recently organized and chaired the controversial PR Week and University of Westminster debate "PR has a duty to tell the truth."

Trevor has a BA Combined Honours in History and Politics from Exeter University and a Postgraduate Certificate in Education from the University of London. He has lectured at the University of Westminster, City University, Exeter University and at Richmond, The American International University.

Married with two daughters, Trevor lives in Battersea, South London. He is a regular theatre goer, keen reader of contemporary fiction and lifelong supporter and season ticket holder of Fulham Football Club.

Simon Goldsworthy, BA Hons

Simon Goldsworthy is Senior Lecturer in Public Communication at the University of Westminster.

He has a first class degree in History from the University of London, and was formerly a member of the UK's Government Information Service, undertaking press and publicity work for a range of government departments, including the Central Office of Information, the Department of Trade and Industry, the Department of Social Security and the Department of the Environment. His duties included advising of government ministers media handling. He subsequently worked both independently and for a number of PR consultancies running PR projects for a wide range of public sector organizations, including an award winning web-based campaign for the UKs largest science research council.

In 2000 Simon launched the first MA program in Public Relations in London at the University of Westminster, adding an undergraduate program two years later. Both programs attract large numbers of students from all over the world, including many parts of Asia, and benefit from excellent links with key figures in the PR industry, many of whom are guest speakers.

Simon has also set up and run courses for universities in other countries, including Johns Hopkins University in the USA, is a regular lecturer at the Sorbonne in Paris, and has acted as consultant and external examiner for a number of PR courses at other UK universities. He has published a range of academic articles, on subjects including PR education and ethics, the relationship between PR and advertising, and aspects of journalism.

Alongside Trevor Morris, Simon took part in the controversial PR and the Truth debate at the University of Westminster, which provoked considerable interest in PR circles internationally, and in a follow-up debate on the same theme at the Sorbonne in Paris.

Simon lives in Chiswick, West London. He is a keen traveler, cinema-goer and reader of history. He is married, with a young son who supports Chelsea Football Club.

Contact: _morrisgoldsworthy@btinternet.com_
(mailto:morrisgoldsworthy@btinternet.com)

Index